STUDIES IN MODERN EUROPEAN LITERATURE
AND THOUGHT

General Editor:
ERICH HELLER
Professor of German
in the University College of Swansea

PAUL CLAUDEL

Other titles are in preparation

PAUL CLAUDEL

BY

WALLACE FOWLIE

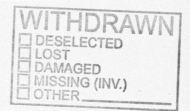
BOWES & BOWES
LONDON

First published in 1957 in the Series
Studies in Modern European Literature and Thought
by Bowes & Bowes Publishers Limited, London

PQ
2605
L36Z67

*Printed in Great Britain
by Richard Clay and Company Ltd,
Bungay, Suffolk*

CONTENTS

I

The Man

Claudel, the poet and dramatist, lived long enough for a public to grow up in his life-time able to comprehend something of the significance of his work. He never ceased to take part in contemporary controversy. From his retreat in Brangues, in the province of Savoy, he sent forth during his last twenty years book after book of scriptural exegesis. He published for more than sixty years and produced one of the most massive contributions to contemporary literature. His is the work of a dialectical intelligence, of a shrewd and determined mind, of a man who lived in many styles, in many countries, and who learned how to reflect deeply on his experience. His two principal modes of knowledge were the intuition of a poet and the theology of a Christian. In all *genres* in which he has written—poems, letters, plays, essays, Biblical exegesis—Claudel steadfastly explored what was for him the central drama: the human soul engaged in its adventure with eternity.

In our time, Catholic theology has hardly inspired a more vehement, more impassioned, and more articulate literary output than Claudel's. Man, World, and God are the key-notes in

7

everything he writes. As he tries to come to terms with his theme, he is absolutistic and imperious. He can be as outspoken and wrathful as Dante was in the thirteenth century. He has a marked predilection for the word 'universe' and for the two related words, 'universality' and 'unity'. From the beginning of his career, his work was consistent. It did not 'develop' in the way characteristic of the works of most literary men.

Despite the high praise from Charles du Bos, who once called him the greatest living genius of the West, and despite the judgment of Jacques Madaule, who compared him with Dante, Paul Claudel's place in literature and in Catholic thought is still vigorously disputed. In his middle eighties, at the time of his death, in February 1955, Claudel appeared as belligerent as ever. He maintained not only his full powers as a writer but also his violent temper and his animosities. His detractors are legion, and his admirers come from many varying quarters, differing widely in their religious, political, and æsthetic beliefs. He has received homage from such writers as the Catholic academician Louis Gillet and the Communist Aragon, from the Protestant Ramuz and the liberal humanist Jean Prévost, from Alain, Maurice Blanchot, and Claudine Chonez. The difficulty of his art explains to some degree the long period of neglect which Claudel suffered. Only since the second World War has there been a marked effort to understand him and to define his position in contemporary literature.

He was born in 1868, in Villeneuve-sur-Fère, a small village in the Tardenois, a locality which lies between the provinces of Ile-de-France and Champagne. Villeneuve today comprises about three hundred families. It lies in one of the rainiest sections of France. A strong wind blows there from the north almost constantly. For many years Claudel maintained contact with the village by spending his vacations there. He always remembered how difficult it was to walk against the wind, and how the church steeple, bent by it, resembled the mast of a schooner. As a child he learned to observe all the details of the countryside. He has written of Nature as he studied her from the highest branch of an old tree he used to climb as a boy. This was the site of his first dialogue with Nature and of his first impressions from which he drew throughout his life. Even at the age of five and six, he was writing what he has called 'kinds of poems'. A real sense of the writer's vocation came to him at thirteen. The poems he wrote at thirteen and fourteen already showed the rhythm and prosody he consciously adopted later. Claudel's family was Catholic in the traditional sense, but not particularly religious or pious.

He received his schooling at the lycée Louis-le-Grand, in Paris. For the young Claudel it was a prison, the stifling atmosphere of which he has described in *Ma Conversion*. Camille Mauclair has recalled the sullen voice of Claudel at the lycée, and his silence, which he would break only to argue with their famous teacher Burdeau. At the graduation ceremonies of 1883 (Claudel was in 'seconde') Renan made the principal address, one that has become celebrated, in which he told the students assembled before him, that the day might come when one of them would denounce him as a corruptor of youth. This prediction was truer than Renan realized, because Claudel never ceased denouncing him. In his last year at Louis-le-Grand, the year of philosophy, Claudel made friends with his classmates: Marcel Schwob, Léon Daudet, Chavannes, the future sinologist.

These were the years when, in company with other young intellectuals, he read Baudelaire and Verlaine. But the first great revelation to Claudel, of both a literary and spiritual order, was Rimbaud. He has described in a passage justly famous and justly disputed the profound effect which the reading of *Les Illuminations* had on him. He first came upon some of the prose poems in the June issue of *La Vogue* of 1886. To him it meant release from what he called the hideous world of Taine, Renan, and the other Molochs of the nineteenth century. 'J'avais la révélation du surnaturel', he wrote to Jacques Rivière. Rimbaud was the vehicle of Claudel's return to his faith. His gratitude is couched in such hyperbolic terms that some critics have wondered whether Claudel, in his letter to Rivière, had not distorted the real facts. A recent critic, Ernest Friche, believes that we can accept Claudel's account, provided we realize that Rimbaud revealed to him enormous poetical potentialities, without, however, imparting a philosophy or even a system of æsthetics. Certain sentences of *Une Saison en Enfer*, such as 'Nous ne sommes pas au monde', never ceased to impress Claudel by clarifying for him the real significance of his own revolt. Claudel was, not unlike Rimbaud himself, a revolutionary, a Dionysian ecstatic. Such prose poems as *Après le Déluge* and *Enfances* taught him something concerning the mysterious character of poetic inspiration preceding personal experiences which were to come later, but which were secretly related to it.

The poet has recorded that in the same year 1886 something else happened to him, something which was to determine his destiny. On Christmas day, in Notre-Dame, during the service of vespers, he experienced a spiritual awakening, a revelation of faith which was never to be impaired or endangered thereafter. In describing this conversion, Claudel speaks of its suddenness and of the perception he had of Divine Innocence. This mystical experience was followed by four years of bewilderment and struggle to harmonize the new force in him with his former self. He began to study the Bible, the history of the Church and its liturgy, and discovered that what he had once valued as poetry was indissolubly associated with religion. He attended Mallarmé's

Tuesday evening gatherings and learned from the master and teacher of symbolism to look at the universe as if it were a text to be deciphered. In his later, somewhat severe article on Mallarmé, *La Catastrophe d'Igitur*, Claudel does acknowledge his debt to the older poet, although he groups Mallarmé with Poe and Baudelaire as a poet of the 'metaphysical night' of the nineteenth century, a poet who lacked the final initiation into the meaning of his art.

At the age of twenty-five, he left for Boston, Massachusetts, to serve there as vice-consul for France. This marked the beginning of a long diplomatic career which took him to many parts of the globe. In China, where he went in 1895, Claudel entered upon a period of solitude, silence, and meditation. His *Vers d'Exil* echo something of the spiritual experience of the five years in China. *Connaissance de l'Est* is a form of intimate journal accompanying the poems. A poem in *Connaissance de l'Est* speaks of one of his returns to Paris, just before leaving for China, when he realized he was unknown in his own country. It constitutes his farewell to his family, his past, his country. He was free and disengaged, ready for the unknown. The physical voyage had its counterpart in a spiritual voyage, comparable to Rimbaud's. Claudel felt no doubts concerning his faith. He had not become a Catholic in order to enjoy religious experience. He had become a Catholic through a sense of obedience, in order to discovery what was demanded of him as a man.

His vocation of a Christian was still obscure to him. He felt himself at the beginning of a diplomatic career, of a writer's career, and of a religious career. All three seemed interrelated, but he was not yet clear as to what was being asked of him.

At Shanghai his consular function occupied all his time apart from attending daily mass, and an hour spent on his own writing. He had greater freedom at Fou-Tcheou and Han-Keou. From these centres he took excursions and observed the landscapes which he recaptured in the pages of *Connaissance de l'Est*. Unlike Mallarmé in his career as teacher, Claudel, who had a highly developed sense of obligation, derived pleasure and satisfaction from his diplomatic and administrative duties. Everything in China interested him: the optimism and good humour of the people, their simplicity and sense of comradeship, their politeness, their art, and their theatre.

His studies in China centred on the Bible and St Thomas Aquinas. Not until the recent book of Ernest Friche, *Etudes Claudéliennes*, has the predominant influence of St Thomas been pointed out. Friche calls Claudel a Thomistic poet. In an important letter, Claudel himself confirmed this influence. 'I read and annotated the two *Summas*,' he wrote. 'It was a wonderful nourishment and training for my mind. Those lessons transformed me and merged with all my creative activity.'

To Rimbaud's doctrine concerning the power of poetic language, and to Mallarmé's doctrine concerning the symbolism of the universe, Claudel added the ambitious synthesis of St Thomas and the religious interpretation of metaphorical language. At the end of the century, when Claudel returned to France from China, he was practising the metaphysical discipline he had acquired from St Thomas without, however, abandoning what he had learned from Rimbaud and Mallarmé.

In September 1900 Claudel entered the Abbey of Ligugé in order to test his religious vocation. He was still undecided about the focus of his life. If he discovered in himself the vocation of a religious, he was ready to give up art and literature. At the monastery of Ligugé he became an oblate of the Benedictine Order, but was discouraged by his superiors from continuing with a religious vocation. He has described how, in his life of prayer at that time, he received a very definite refusal, a 'No' which came to him in a semi-mystical way. In his poem, *Sainte Thérèse*, Claudel describes the religious vocation in which the will of God is substituted for man's will. A priest is not necessarily prevented from writing poems, but poetry cannot be the principal goal of his life. In the deepest sense, for Claudel, there is incompatibility between the priesthood and the poet's calling. For him the debate was settled in 1900.

As ambassador, Claudel represented France in Tokyo, Washington, and Brussels. His diplomatic career, which included posts in Prague, Frankfurt, Hamburg, Rio de Janeiro, kept him away from France and literary groups. His travels helped to make him into one of the most universal of French writers. The scope of his interests and studies is unusual for a French poet: Chinese theatre, Italian and Dutch painting, Japanese poetry, Spanish culture, and English Catholic literature, some of which he has translated. The last years of his life he spent in Brangues. He went to Paris for the new productions of his plays: *Le Soulier de Satin* in 1943, *Partage de Midi* in 1948, *L'Annonce faite à Marie* in 1955, just before his death.

Between the years spent in China at the end of the century and the performances of *L'Annonce faite à Marie* in 1912 not much public attention was focused on Claudel, and even from his friends on the *Nouvelle Revue Française*, which published his work from 1909 on, he heard very little. Their admiration was silent. Gide and Rivière both had marked admiration for Claudel, but failed to express it at that time. A few critics, Souday and Pierre Lasserre especially, attacked him. Even later in his career, Claudel suffered from the silence of the critics and the public. *Le Soulier de Satin* was scarcely noticed when it was first published. Not a single notice or review of *Corona Benignitatis Anni Dei* appeared. And even in recent years his books of Biblical exegesis are still largely neglected. This paucity of critical notice is perhaps due to intimidation or a sense of embarrassment on the part of the critics. They are unusual books, difficult to review and evaluate. Very slowly the public is growing used to Claudel's language and thought. He died a great figure, but an ill-known figure.

As a writer, Claudel never made concessions to his public. The Catholic world in France and outside of France has been slow to accept him. When he presented his candidacy for the Académie Française just before the war, he failed to win the election. Not until after the war, in 1946, was he invited to become a member of the group. His attitude towards the world of letters, and even towards the world in general, has seemed hostile and almost vindictive. His implacable seriousness has discouraged any sense of humour. He has the temperament of a stubborn peasant, comparable in this respect to Péguy. And yet Claudel has participated gladly in every aspect of the Catholic revival in France: in art, philosophy, and liturgy. His obvious disdain for many of his contemporaries and for the younger writers has not prevented his influence from deeply affecting the lives of some. His early correspondence with Jacques Rivière revealed his exceptional powers as apologist and defender of the faith. The publication, in 1949, of the correspondence between Gide and Claudel was an event of great importance. This exchange of letters belongs primarily to the realm of apologetics and criticism. Exchanges of letters in this century have reflected perhaps more succinctly than any other form of writing the spiritual problems of the age:

16

for instance, the correspondence between Jacques Rivière and Alain-Fournier, between Rivière and Claudel, between Gide and Francis Jammes, between Gide and Claudel.

By virtue of his strength, his consistent serious-ness, and the proportions of his work, Claudel towers above his contemporaries. As he remains outside all literary coteries, his presence has been felt by its sheer spiritual weight.

Despite Claudel's often-expressed scorn for much of the literature of the nineteenth century ('A desert covered with ruins and excavations,' he once called it), he has always maintained respect for some of its greatest figures—Baudelaire, Ver-laine, Rimbaud, Balzac—and has described the period between 1830 and 1870 as imaginatively the most powerful since the Middle Ages. He has done justice to Hugo, appreciating the vitality of his rhetoric, the richness and colour of his language. Yet Hugo is far from being for him the supreme type of poet; this role is played by Shakespeare, Dante, and Virgil.

In the recent interviews with Jean Amrouche, *Mémoires Improvisés*, Claudel states that he has al-ways been an omnivorous reader. He repudiated in its entirety the literary training he received at school. During the four or five years following his conversion in 1886 he taught himself, follow-ing an ambitious programme of reading which centred on Shakespeare, whose influence is con-spicuous in the imagery, rhythm, and form of the first version of *Tête d'Or*. He learned to read

Æschylus and the other Greeks in the original. The iamb he believed the form best suited to dramatic composition. Racine, who used the classical alexandrine line of twelve syllables, is an exception for Claudel. He hated Racine when he first studied him at the lycée; only after many years he came to understand and feel the greatness of *Britannicus*, *Phèdre*, and *Athalie*. And as, much later, his admiration for Shakespeare decreased, Racine for him grew in stature. Dante he places very high among poets, and Virgil above all others. To Dostoievski he owes a great deal; he once called him the inventor of 'polymorphous characters'. Dostoievski provided him with countless examples of the unforeseen, the unknown element in human nature. Claudel himself never thought of writing a novel. The form is foreign to his temperament. Balzac and Dostoievski were the novelists he most admired. He read part of Proust's novel, but with marked distaste. He disliked Stendhal and was puzzled by the glory that has come to him. Aristotle and St Thomas Aquinas were his two principal philosophers. His debt to Bossuet was both theological and artistic. Claudel's language, in its sonorous melodic quality, owes as much to Bossuet as to Rimbaud. His judgment about Pascal was reserved; Pascal's silence on the two subjects of the Virgin and the Eucharist led Claudel to doubt his importance as a Catholic thinker. Montaigne he frankly disliked and did not read.

Like every Christian, Claudel is simultaneously optimistic and pessimistic. Goodness can be achieved in this world, but only through suffering. Fundamentally, he does not believe in the temporal triumph of the Church. Persecution, he reminds us, is one of the promises of Christ. Claudel appears today as a patriarch contemplating the evil and chaos of our planet. His attitude towards much of contemporary literature is sullen and vindictive. In speaking of Jean-Paul Sartre and Existentialists, he said, 'How can they live in that atmosphere of cafés, of drunkenness and pederasty?' He often appears as the solitary judge of our day, one of the most serious of contemporary writers. His diction remained unaffected by any particular fashion or coterie. It is solid and varied. It has elements of the sermon in it, but also elements of Gothic richness. His verse is more flexible and more sensuous than the alexandrine. He understood Valéry's position and Valéry's faith in the alexandrine, but he claimed that it did not correspond to his own particular need of expression. He has rigorously opposed the view of Valéry and Gide that beauty is the result of constraint and limitation.

It is impossible to claim for Claudel any one specific role in contemporary French literature. He is many things at once. His feeling for organic life, for the robustness and resources of the human body will remind Americans of Walt Whitman. His favourite type of adventurer-hero, Tête d'Or or Don Camille, shows some of the traits of a Hemingway hero. On the other hand, his adaptations of *Les Choéphores*, *Les Euménides*, and *Agamemnon* have the ceremonial rigour of the earliest Greek tragedies. More than any other Frenchman, Claudel has revealed the Orient to his country: China and Japan especially. He has liberated the French theatre from the monotonous dialogue of the realists. In many instances the poetic language of his own plays is too difficult to permit theatrical production, but his example has helped contemporary French audiences to follow the language of Giraudoux, Lorca, and Eliot.

Always guided by his Catholicism, Claudel has created and re-created, interpreted and modified an endless number of myths and ideas. Man is for him at all times equally flesh and spirit, expressing in his duality the mystery of the Incarnation. Men in all parts of the world, in the remotest districts and in the metropolitan centres, are all sharing in the same existence and experiencing the drama of an identical destiny. In his role of poet, Claudel has enlarged life for his readers by encompassing many countries and their histories.

Not all the books of Claudel possess the lyric sublimity of *Cinq Grandes Odes* or *L'Annonce faite à Marie*. Some, such as *Un Poète regarde la Croix*, are mere reservoirs of symbols and 'correspondences'. Never contaminated by the Jansenism of his period, which has weakened so much contemporary Catholic literature, Claudel has always been free from prudery and narrow-mindedness. He has opened himself to the universe ('consentir à l'univers') in what he calls a marriage with the universe in the heart of Christ. He considers the Cross as the true meeting-place between God and His creation. At the moment of the Cross the creation participated in all suffering and all exaltation.

In his acceptance of the world, which is not pantheistic but the expression of his striving for unity, Claudel remained always a dedicated son of the Church. Without reservations or explanations, he never missed an opportunity to declare himself a Catholic. This has often embarrassed readers who do not share his belief. Claudel's faith was far from being an æsthetic, or, for that matter, any other sort of 'attitude'. It represented for him the one truth. But he has often explained that the Catholic lives in a world of harsh reality, where his life becomes a continuous effort, where life itself is constantly at stake. The Catholic faith is easy to give up. It is extraordinarily difficult to return to it and live by it again. In his essays and religious meditations, Claudel often reveals a profound spirit of humility. He makes an effort to understand, but also acknowledges defeat in the face of the unknowable. He attacks that literary realism which claims to be concerned with 'truth'. Scholarship, the notebook, the case history furnish, according to Claudel, a very small amount of knowledge about man, by comparison with what the mystics have bequeathed us. Taken as a whole, his work is praise to God and praise to His creation. It does not reflect the exaltation of a mystic, but it is rather the expression of the natural joy of a man who has found an order in the universe and believes in a certain relationship between this world and eternity.

II

The Poet

At the beginning of his career Claudel wrote extensively about his theory of poetry, and he continued at frequent intervals to add to this theoretical part of his writing. The additional observations show no divergence from the early doctrine. Right from the outset Claudel was sure of his æsthetic and philosophical beliefs. The tenets of his *Art Poétique* have been substantiated, confirmed, and repeated rather than enlarged or modified. In his interviews of 1953 with Jean Amrouche, the octogenarian poet restated some of his basic convictions which he had expressed as early as the turn of the century.

As a poet he wants to define his purpose by stating his relationship to the world, to God, and to himself. This point of departure in terms of relationship or analogy is the lesson bequeathed to him by Mallarmé, who had become for Claudel not the great modern poet but the great teacher of modern poets. The *Art Poétique* was not the result of introspection. Claudel claims that he seldom indulges in what is called today introspective thinking. Finding exterior problems far more interesting, he opposes the Socratic maxim of 'Know thyself'. The world is an immense subject-matter awaiting the poet who will be able to reveal its meaning. This belief would be very consistent with Mallarmé's. But when Claudel continues by equating the revelation of this meaning with an act of grace, he passes beyond the æsthetics of Mallarmé. Knowledge is not a submission to the object, but a victory over it. The word, as used by the poet, is a condensation of the energy of sentiment. It preserves the power of sentiment, indeed it creatively enhances it, and ultimately transforms it into a power capable of illuminating the world.

By temperament, Claudel was hardly disposed to accept the rule and the model of other poets. His poetic practice may be reminiscent to some degree of Mallarmé and Rimbaud, but he forces and affirms his subject far more than they do. The desire to communicate the universal, the cosmically universal, made him cultivate his sense of discipline and hierarchy. As a poet, he loves speaking *ex cathedra*. The Claudelian verse conveys something of the heart-beat and the breath of the poet reciting. It waxes, reaches a climax, and wanes in a style that is natural, oral, and primitive. The lyric intention of a Claudel poem is identifiable with its being read aloud.

In his letter to Henri Bremond on the controversial concept of 'pure poetry', Claudel acknowledges his belief that poetry is the work of a faculty in man which bears closer relationship to imagination and sensibility than to reason. And yet reason, taste, a sense of proportion, have their part in the creative process. They intervene after the exercise of the first faculty. Poetry, in the simplest definition which Claudel has given, is the effect of a certain need in man to make something, to realize with words the idea that he had concerning something. A vocation is necessary. A poet is a 'man called'. Inspiration itself is a rhythmical excitement, a sense of verbal order, with the faculties of the poet in a state of exceptional attentiveness and concentration. As breath precedes voice, so the desire to express precedes the expression.

Claudel revives and restates some of the oldest and noblest claims for the poetic genius. He implies that simply by listening to the voice of the poet we are initiated into the mysteries of the universe. Before we necessarily understand the words themselves of the poet, we participate in their meaning. The work of the poet rises up from such profound sources that it is comparable to an element of nature. We follow first the ineffable part of poetry, because it is in harmony with creation. We recognize it without understanding it, and we listen to it as we listen to the music of seas and rivers.

At the beginning of *La Ville* (2nd version), the character Besme speaks to the poet Cœuvre and tells him of the effect of the poet's words on other men, of the experience of peace which follows after thought:

Car, quand tu parles, comme un arbre qui de
    toute sa feuille
S'émeut dans le silence de Midi, la paix en nous
    peu à peu succède à la pensée.

A poem is no more an 'explanation' than a flower
is, or a hillside or a sunset. It is that which
'means' by its form, its beauty, its wholeness.

Tu n'expliques rien, ô poète, mais toutes choses
    par toi nous deviennent explicables.

The poet is the man able to release the secret
potentialities of a word which in ordinary speech
is a purely conventional sign. The sound of the
word, when it becomes audible in the poet's
verse, restores a kind of existence to the object it
names. The object is thus recreated, but not
necessarily explained. The words, by their place
and their sound, in the poet's verse, find a new
meaning simply through the order of their
arrangement. The action of the poet seems,
therefore, magical or supernatural. He calls
words into being and finds for them a new life
in the new complexity of their arrangement.

Each line of the poet is a new creation, according to Claudel, but it cannot be separated from
the line which precedes it and the line which
comes after it. Art closely follows the principle
of Nature in its continuousness, in its constant
development, in its pattern of unfolding. Each
minute in time alters the composition of the
world, and in the same way each line of a poem,

as it is said, alters the design of the poem and even the design and the intention of the entire work of the poet. An event in life does not eradicate all other events, and a new flower bursting into bloom does not efface all other flowers. In the same way, a new line in a poem, or indeed a new poem, does not replace other lines and other poems, but exists with them in a constantly renewed creation.

In his definition of metaphor, which Claudel claims to be the basis of his art, he calls it a new word, a joining of two different things. A metaphor is the poet's creation because in it he brings about a *rapprochement* which has not been realized in nature. In his treatise, *Connaissance du Temps*, Claudel characterizes this operation of metaphor as the poet's testimony to the constant 'primitive-ness' of the world, to the principle of modulation and change by which the world continues to exist. Two things which seemingly were moving in opposite directions, without any relationship between them, are suddenly and unexpectedly joined. Father Walter Ong, in his analysis of Shakespeare's *The Phoenix and the Turtle*, calls this operation 'the twinning aspect of metaphor' (*Sewanee Review*, Spring 1955), and argues that the two parts of the metaphor are destined to be coupled. 'They generate truth only by pairing with one another.'

The thought of Claudel is expressed in images and metaphors which seem to generate them-selves in the most natural and abundant way.

They are everywhere, sensual images of light and sound and feeling, containing the thought and proffering it without any abstraction. To understand by images is a characteristic of primitive man. The fullness which Claudel feels in life is translated directly into the spontaneous welling up of images, in the naturalness of the rhythm of his lines which coincide exactly with the breathing of the poet. The emotion of the line controls its meter, which expands or contracts in accord with the intensity of the emotion. This system, unique in the history of French prosody, was fully applied in the earliest poems (*Cinq Grandes Odes*) and the earliest plays of Claudel (*Tête d'Or*). The appearance of the line on the page, its brevity or its excessive length, is an indication of its emotional content. The plethora of images in Claudel's poetry expresses his profound feeling for the continuity of life, and the varied rhythms of the separate lines reproduce the breathing of the poet and the heart-beat.

As the body of his poetic work increased, Claudel's doctrine concerning the world, the poet, and God was deepened and enriched. As the work expanded, the doctrine, which was intact at the beginning, expanded likewise. But since it was doctrine based on revelation, it can hardly be put into a system and annotated. The image of a 'tree', which Claudel used at the beginning as the general title of his plays, is the image of growth which possesses at all times unity and perfection. When, in a short treatise, *Abrégé de Toute la Doctrine Chrétienne*, Claudel did attempt to 'deduce' his doctrine and organize and expound it, it lost much of the strength and fullness which it always maintains in his creative works.

If we examine the world as we should, that is, in its totality, in the reality of its multiple relationships, we shall then begin to feel the laws which control its existence. If we define one object in the world, we isolate and immobilize it, and hence we falsify it because no one thing exists alone. The world is a unity, for Claudel, and so much a part of universal harmony that it is ineffable. Man tends to analyse a subject in order to understand it, but the action of time, the continuing of the world and of the worlds, contradicts his effort.

The very basis of Claudel's dramaturgy lies in this vision of the world's unity. The world itself is a drama in which something is happening at every instant of time. His statement in *Traité de la Connaissance du Monde et de Soi-même*, which has upset the philologists, is explicit. 'Nous ne sommes pas seuls. Naître, pour tout, c'est conaître. Toute naissance est une connaissance.' This comes about, according to Claudel's cosmology, because all spirit and all matter are in constant movement. 'Tout est mouvement.' The struggle of each moment within its limitations is a force creating form. 'La vibration, c'est le mouvement prisonnier de la forme.' Hence the universe is being constantly created, with each part in relationship with and in knowledge of all other parts.

Whereas animals have only a sensory knowledge of the universe, man has an intellectual knowledge. He can recognize himself in any part of the universe and adjust himself to many conditions. His existence is realized through all those things in the world he 'knows'. He gives them meaning and relates them one to the other. Through him the universe is expressed. He participates in the ceaseless flow and change of the universe. He is the microcosm of the world, its 'host'. 'Il est des choses l'image comprenante, et consommante, l'hostie intelligible en qui elles sont consommées.' His very understanding of the world is its presentation as a drama. Claudel calls man both witness and actor of the same drama-spectacle. He is part of the world's performance, one of the world's chorus, and yet his work is a development of this very performance.

From this metaphor describing man's function and role, Claudel derives his definition of crime and evil. It is man's withdrawal from the chorus of the world, his will to renounce his own character and to vitiate his natural tendencies. When he renounces his part in the chorus, he loses his sense of constancy and order. This image we also find in Plotinus, in the sixth *Ennead*. It is the basis of *Cinq Grandes Odes*, especially the opening *Muses*, and it pervades the dramas, where the will to disobedience is described as dormant in man's heart, a will to exert the power of freedom for the wrong reasons. A breaking of the law, which is a breaking of man's pact with the world and with God, is both possible, because of its daily occurrence, and impossible, because it cannot persist for long. The world ultimately is able to reestablish its harmony. We are protagonists in a ceremonial drama far greater than ourselves, and are able to leave it only momentarily.

Claudel explores this concept of ceremony and movement in his discovery and definition of God. The poet sees every created thing in perpetual movement. We move by coming into contact with all the other things in the world. By this constant movement we waste ourselves and finally perish. 'Tout périt. L'Univers n'est qu'une manière totale de ne pas être ce qui est.' Existing within this movement, we unconsciously tend to deny that which is constant. This is our separation from God. Yet while Nature is a constant combining of forms all of which are capable of perishing, the end is for Claudel, in *Traité de la Connaissance*, unity or oneness or a return to God whence it all came originally.

The human spirit alone is able to comprehend something of the bond which exists between the instability of the world and the stability of God. By naming an object, as the poet does, man rescues it from its fate of dissolution. In *Traité de la Connaissance* Claudel reaches a definition of man and of the poet as the one whose function is to *represent* (or reproduce) the creation of the

Creator. 'Tout passe, et, rien n'étant présent, tout doit être *représenté*.' All the parts of the world find in man, in the incorruptible part of man, an intelligence which understands them and which is able to offer them to the One who created them in the beginning. The poet Paul Claudel believes that every man is in some sense a poet.

The *Odes* of Claudel lack the ordered regularity and the calculated development which are associated with the classical ode. The wealth of imagery and scenes and ideas prevents any facile organization. All the elements of the ode seem to be uttered simultaneously. Each ode is comparable to a long, continuous sentence which may be interrupted at any point by the sudden rising up of an image. Within the poem itself, the poet speaks of its creation, of its will to grow by itself in its constant adaptation to the thought and the emotions of the poet. Each word calls up another word. Their movement is presided over by the imagination rather than by the intellect. Only the imagination is able to relate the varied images. The poet warns the grammarian not to look for 'logical' relationships in the poems, but to find their centre.

O grammarien dans mes vers! Ne cherche point le chemin, cherche le centre! (*Les Muses*)

Yet Claudel insists that thought, thought of a certain order, pervades each ode from beginning to end, although it is never in full view. Claudel's poetry tries to demonstrate poetically the nature of the cosmos, the need which each element in it has of all the others.

The *Art Poétique* is made up of two treatises, the first, *Connaissance du Temps*, written in 1903, and the second, *Connaissance du Monde et de Soi-même*, written in 1904. They are presented in doctrinal, didactic form, but they are also a profession of faith and represent a conclusion to many of the æsthetic beliefs of Baudelaire, Rimbaud, and Mallarmé. In a letter to Père Angers, who published in 1949 an annotated critical edition of the *Art Poétique*, Claudel says that for fifty years he has been *living* the *Art Poétique*. His conversion of 1886 was followed by the struggle and labour of a life-time. In purely spiritual terms, his entire work is a progression towards the consciousness of the 'Real Presence' in the world. Poetic experience is only one stage in this progression. Another stage is prayer. A still higher stage is adoration.

All the parts of Claudel's vast work are inter-related. *Connaissance de l'Est* was a kind of sketch-book for the *Art Poétique*. The *Odes*, written after the *Art Poétique*, repeat and orchestrate themes of the treatises. The early plays, grouped under the title *L'Arbre*, deal with spiritual problems which find to some extent their solution in the later plays.

In the miracle of metaphor a kind of answer to two questions is reached: a reason for the world and a reason for man. In his doctrine concerning the poetic word which transmits an image of the relationship of things, Claudel's debt to Rimbaud is obvious. The world is limitless in its relationships, and the poet, in his role of conqueror of the poetic word, becomes reader of the world and decipherer of its relationships. The two most widely separated terms of metaphor are for Claudel the World and God. In making poetic speech into the means of joining these two extremes, he was applying logically the dual revelation which came to him from his early reading of Rimbaud and his religious experience of Christmas 1886. Even in the physical conquest of the earth, in the campaigns inspired apparently by the mere will to power, there is a deeply spiritual reason. The ambition of the poet, in his will to know the world, is not unrelated to the ambition of the conqueror.

The universe is looked upon as an *ensemble*, conceived in the same way as the work of the artist is conceived. 'Chaque chose dans un rapport infini avec les autres.' From the mineral to the angelic, every element has secret affinities with every other element. In accord with the great symbolic tradition of the Middle Ages, all the forms in the world are believed to be symbols of Divine Essence. Yet man remains sovereign and free even when he is moved by those mysterious forces which animate and re-create the world. Man exists in order to know. He knows in two ways : objectively, by what he calls positivistic science; and subjectively or intuitively, when, while contemplating the world, he feels the eye of his Creator upon him. Thus he exists as an intermediary being between the Creator and the creation, and his knowledge, in its fullest sense, becomes an instrument of salvation, a progress towards order and the regaining of a lost happiness.

Claudel repudiates the doctrine of art for art's sake. The poet, for him, is not the creator of the beautiful; his task is rather, existing as he does as a creature, to realize the totality of the universe, to discover the meaning of its drama, and to pay homage to the Creator. The system of Claudel is a dialectics of analogy, the key to which is to be found in Holy Scripture. This theory of Claudel, as developed in the *Introduction au Livre de Ruth*, parallels that of the Fathers of the Church. Everything in the visible world bears a relationship to the invisible.

The living, moving things around us are signs and symbols of the life of the spirit. The poet celebrates Nature by realizing these analogies between the two realms; and as the spirit is omnipresent, everything that is 'present' to the poet has to be accepted by him in all its vitality, profusion, and even brutality. Claudel, therefore, rejects the familiar romantic themes of nostalgia for the past, for dreams and flights from reality.

Claudel's cosmological belief is reflected in his chosen poetic form: in the vital rhythm of his free verse. We do not think and we do not live in an even, continuous way. There are breaks, pauses, and interventions in our ideas, our notions, our memories. The art of Claudel succeeds pre-eminently in preserving something of the roughness, the harshness and the unevenness of existence, of the spiritual tension which antedates the actual poem. This tension has indeed been artistically transformed, but its substance remains unchanged, as a stone that has been cut preserves its 'stoniness'.

Mais vous m'avez placé dans la terre, afin que
    j'endure la gêne et l'étroitesse et l'obscurité,
Et la violence de ces autres pierres qui sont
    appuyées sur moi,
Et que j'occupe ma place pour toujours comme
    une pierre taillée qui a sa forme et son poids.
            (*La Muse qui est la Grâce*)

This passage, among countless others, defines Claudel's term *connaissance* as being the response of man's entire being to the shock of the exterior world. And in reverse order, the world itself reaches its culmination in man who is within the world.

Symbolism is the centre of Claudel's poetic achievement. Since visible reality is the image of invisible reality, the poet is able to establish a relationship between the Creator and the created world. The meaning of each thing is the image it gives of God. The universe is a complicated network of metaphors, of which the primordial metaphor is man himself who was created in the image of God. In its fundamental spirituality, the symbolic system of Claudel is closely related to mediæval symbolism. Symbolism, for him, is quite literally one way of understanding God. The poet learns how to create in himself a silence wherein he reaches a state of freedom, a total attentiveness to grace. This subject is movingly developed in the ode, *L'Esprit et l'Eau*. The breath of the spirit fills the poet and dictates his poems to him. He prays to be granted the word that is fully intelligible:

Et moi qui fais les choses éternelles avec ma voix,
    faites que je sois tout entier
Cette voix, une parole totalement intelligible!

The universe is conceived as constantly soliciting the poet to speak, to give a verbal articulation to the vast *ensemble* of things which exist together.

For Paul Valéry, the principal discovery of symbolism was the concept of 'pure poetry'. The goal of Mallarmé had been to purge poetry of all didactic, utilitarian, and moralistic elements. This goal, and the symbolist belief that poetry should be incantation, were acceptable to Claudel despite the importance of his religious faith, which has set him apart from the symbolist movement proper. Claudel's vision of the world in its fullness and inexhaustible richness was destined to alienate him from Mallarmé's poetic experience. Mallarmé's world seen as *grimoire*, as a conjuror's book of magic recipes, where the art of poetry was the rigorous exercise of purification and reduction, became Claudel's experience of the world as Logos, and of poetry as a means of celebrating the love of God. However, Claudel's debt to symbolism, and especially to Rimbaud, is tremendous. Rimbaud's initial impulse, strongly guided by Baudelaire's æsthetics, had been to make of the poetic word an instrument of discovery. Claudel learned from the example of Baudelaire and Rimbaud the lesson of 'pure receptivity', a state in which language will be far less an expression through words than a revelation of meaning through symbols. Words, rising up almost fortuitously from the subconscious or from the secret depths of the poet's consciousness, will, on their own accord, produce the particular medium of communication that is, in fact, poetry. The new poetic style, which the *Odes* of Claudel illustrate more brilliantly than any other poetic work of our time, reflects the texture of thought at the very moment of its conception. The ambition of Rimbaud was to be simultaneously *voyant* and creator, visionary, and poet. His work is composed of the hallucinations he induced in himself and the record of his failure. The example of his attempt to reach the integrity of primitive man and know the fascination of all things in the world was one of Claudel's great inspirations. In his poetic practice he differs radically from Rimbaud, but he has remained extraordinarily close to Rimbaud in his effort to suppress all forms of 'approximate' language and to achieve through the poetic word an identification of subject-matter and verbal expression. The history of French poetry during the past one hundred years has been the exploration of the 'profound unity' first stated by Baudelaire in his sonnet on *Correspondances* and amplified and celebrated by Claudel in his *Odes*. Creation is an *ensemble* of figures and signs to be deciphered. The role of the poet is precisely that of expressing the unity of the universe as it is reflected in his soul. The words of the poet are not generalizations. They are concrete and individual, assembled in order to bring about the fusion between language and reality.

Thus Claudel transformed into his own religious symbolism the symbolist practice of Baudelaire, Rimbaud, and Mallarmé. Even the symbol of 'The Tree' (*Arbre*), the name which Claudel gave to his first five plays, carries religious connotations: the cross or sign of salvation; the annual dying for the sake of growth; the steadfastness of faith and fidelity. Claudel's sense of vocation as a religious poet, fully expressed in the *Cinq Grandes Odes*, was inspired by what he believed to be mystical intuitions in the writings of Rimbaud, and by the lesson of Mallarmé, who had taught him to ask such questions as 'what is the meaning of a tree?'

A footnote to the first ode, *Les Muses* (written in 1900 and 1904, at the time of the *Art Poétique*), indicates that the poet is contemplating a sarcophagus, first discovered on the road of Ostia and today housed in the Louvre.* On the sarcophagus is a representation of the nine Muses. Terpsichore, holding the centre, is the first evoked by the poet. She is the Muse of Dance and Choral Singing. She is movement, and the sculptor has depicted her with one arm raised as if she were impatient to begin the dance to the rhythm of music. She is necessary to her eight sisters because movement is the source of life. She presides over the rotation of celestial bodies as well as over the beating of each heart. With her invocation the poem begins. The poet next turns to Mnemosyne who is the Muse of Memory. She is able to relate the poet to time. She reminds him of three guiding poets of the past: Homer, poet of Greece; Virgil, poet of the Roman Empire; Dante, poet of Christendom. But the living poet feels no need to be guided historically or didactically. He turns away from them with the knowledge that the drama he is undergoing is his own. The Muses themselves will only serve as moderators in this experience. 'Toute route à suivre nous ennuie,' he says as he turns away from each great poet of the past, and:

> O mon âme! le poëme n'est point fait de ces lettres que je plante comme des clous, mais du blanc qui reste sur le papier.

* Jean Seznec has written an essay on *Les Muses*, published in *Perspectives of Criticism*, edited by Harry Levin (Harvard University Press). I have profited from a brilliant analysis and interpretation of *Les Muses*, written by Arthur Evans, which is as yet unpublished.

Thalia, Muse of Comedy, and Clio, Muse of History, offer to the poet the spectacles of life, in the form of drama and history. Thalia is a provider of material for the poet. Her mask is the comic, a formula for transmutation. Clio is the writer, the recorder. By inscribing the shadow actions of man, she confers authenticity on his actions. These four sisters, taken together, assist at the moment of poetic inspiration, and exert a secret influence on the poet. Their gifts are not unlike those of the Holy Spirit.

The second group is formed by the 'Inspired' or the 'Intelligent' Muses, who will help to compose the song out of the poet's cry. Euterpe, Muse of Music and Poetry, holds the lyre. She represents the moment of transition from the idea of the poem to the beginning of its composition. But the lyre is not sufficient by itself. Urania, Muse of Astronomy, has to assist because she brings with her a sense of order and system. Melpomene, at the extreme end of the long sarcophagus, is the Muse of Tragedy. She stands in a position opposite to Clio's, and, like her, teaches that a poem is an imitation of human action. Her role is to unify and harmonize all the elements of the poem. She once presided over the tragedies of Sophocles and the odes of Pindar, over the story of Oedipus and the victory of the naked athlete. In the midst of her sisters stands Polymnia, the veiled Muse of Sacred Poetry. She is the voice of the poet in its primitive purity. She is witness to reality. When the poet calls her

'Servant of God, full of grace,' we realize that she is a Mary-figure. She co-operates in the maintenance of the universe, as the poet co-operates by uttering the name of each thing.

Ainsi quand tu parles, ô poëte, dans une énu-
    meration délectable
Proférant de chaque chose le nom,
Comme un père tu l'appelles mystérieusement
    dans son principe, et selon que jadis
Tu participas à sa création, tu coopères à son
    existence!
Toute parole une répétition.

The appearance of Erato, last Muse and guardian of Lyric Poetry, is abrupt and fiery. She in her nudity is all things at once: dance, music, song. She is the one for whom the poet has been waiting and whom he will follow henceforth. She is intoxication, far stronger and far more imperious than the intoxication of wine. She comes in the role of the betrothed, because she will lead the poet away from the world.

Ne sens-tu point ma main sur ta main? (Et en
    effet, je sentis, je sentis sa main sur ma main!)

She brings with her the poet's liberation from the world. With her as his support, he will abandon all that is inferior to his new vocation. Poetry is a necessity. In *Les Muses*, the prologue ode, Claudel tells us the origin of his new allegiance.

The subsequent odes are dramas of purification

and realization. Because the poetic state is unity, he will experience in its rational, irrational, and supernatural powers. It is impossible to analyze these poems solely in terms of the metaphysical and æsthetic problems they suggest. They involve much more.

The second ode, *L'Esprit et l'Eau*, Claudel wrote in Pekin, within the walls of the ancient city, himself feeling a captive there. This literal captivity symbolizes to him others: the captivity of the children of Israel and the captivity of the Church Militant. The idea of liberation comes to him in the image of the sea. The freedom of the waters stands for the freedom of the spirit. The analogy between water and spirit is based upon the fact that neither one can be contained. But this very freedom, unless it leads the poet towards his Creator, will constitute a grave danger.

O mon Dieu, mon être soupire vers le vôtre!
Délivrez-moi de moi-même! délivrez l'être de la condition!
Je suis libre, délivrez-moi de la liberté!

The poet at first suffers from the distance between himself and God. He feels his captivity in the world, in time, in his own being. But this particular meditation leads him to one of his cardinal beliefs, discussed as theory in the *Art Poétique* and now fully articulated in this ode. The world is finite, but God is in it. Man is nowhere if he is not with God.

Vous êtes en ce monde visible comme dans
l'autre.
Vous êtes ici et je ne puis pas être autre part
qu'avec vous.

The world appears new and whole to the poet
when he realizes that the continuity between it
and the invisible world is maintained by the
spirit. Possessing the qualities of water, the spirit
infiltrates everywhere. Each object in the world
signifies the totality of the world. Every being is
the work of eternity. In this state of illumination,
the poet's voice can speak only eternal words.

Step by step, the poet traces the way to holiness: the memory of sin which indicates that his
purification is not complete, the need to know
human love before acceding to divine love which
may be obscured. The penitential theme is
strong in this ode and many of the passages are
reminiscent of Claudel's greatest penitential play,
Partage de Midi. At the end of the experience the
poet has been saved as from a tempest. He is
alone, facing the wisdom of God, which appears
to him as a 'tower of glory and a crowned queen'.

The next poem, the *Magnificat*, is the ode of
thanksgiving, patterned on the words of the Virgin spoken at the home of Elizabeth. At the
beginning of the poem, Claudel recalls his eigh-
teenth year and his return to Notre-Dame on
Christmas Day, where he listened to the singing
of the first *Magnificat*. Now he is thirty-nine, and
living in the same kind of silence he spoke of at

the end of the second ode. But now the highest joy was granted to him. What he solicits is the power to sing of this joy, to articulate it, to offer it as praise and love. The poet's way to God is the act of embracing all things. It is not the direct way of the mystic. The experience of fatherhood which Claudel sings of in this ode permits him to see the work of creation as an aspect of paternity.

The following ode, *La Muse qui est la grâce*, is a theological answer to the *Magnificat* and reflects at the same time Claudel's profound insight into the nature of poetic inspiration. Inspiration is described in the introduction as an invasion of the soul by a force foreign to the poet. He is in a state of such frenzy that the words he will use will not be the same as those of every day. After this introduction, the ode, constructed in the form associated with the names of Pindar and Ronsard, contains three strophes and anti-strophes, followed by an epode where the poet speaks directly as he does in the introduction.

Strophe I. The dialogue begins.* The strophe is the speech of the poet, as the antistrophe is the answer of the Muse. It is the old debate between the flesh and the spirit, between nature and grace. The poet is abrupt and almost impertinent in his speech to the Muse. He wants to be alone and tries to send her away as one would a child.

* Leo Spitzer has published a detailed analysis of this first strophe in *Linguistics and Literary History*, Princeton University Press, 1948.

Va-t-en de moi un peu! laisse-moi faire ce que je
  veux un peu.

He wants a useful place in the world, a role comparable to a builder of railroads or a trade-union
leader. He wants to encompass in his poems all
the works of men, showing how necessary every
simple function is in the totality of society.

Je chanterai le grand poème de l'homme sous-
  trait au hasard!

Antistrophe I. The first answer of the Muse is
a strong rebuke. He has not understood their
relationship. She is a woman, and all his reason-
ings and plans are ludicrous in terms of the immortality she is conferring upon him. Naked as
a god and crowned with vine branches, he is to
leap upon the stage, where he will be once again
Dionysos.

Strophe II. But the poet resists. He cannot yet
see what she wants him to see. He still lives in
the darkness of his mind, in a darkness which he
calls the privation of God. His gift is the cry of
a man, and he is trying to understand the meaning
of the cry.

Antistrophe II. She knows that he has not yet
guessed who she is. His first lesson must be that
of sorrow before he is able to bear the knowledge
of her full name and the fullness of her joy. From
now onwards he will limp because she has
wounded him.

Strophe III. He accepts the wound and the

sorrow, and with them he accepts the knowledge that he must give all. He will not be complete until he answers her call, because,

Antistrophe III—although she is the Muse, her other name is Grace. Before the poet can become the liberator of men, he must liberate himself. If he gives himself, he will be given the entire world. The poet has to obey simultaneously the call of the world and the call of the Muse. The work of accomplishment is at the same time the work of destruction. At the high point of noon, all is exterminated by fire.

Epode. The poet cannot yet bear the idea of the flame. Again, as at the beginning, he wards off the 'Muse who is Grace' and returns to the cool earth where he will not be consumed, and to his ancient sister of darkness, his spouse of the night. He followed the Muse as far as the blossoming and rich promise of spring, but he was not able to accept the holocaust of summer.

The last ode, *La Maison Fermée*, opens with the people's accusation of the poet. He has betrayed them and failed in his mission. They ask him to justify himself. Another dialogue is introduced between the poet's guardian and the poet. She claims that his present solitude is necessary and that he has no more duties towards the people who clamour for his word. The poet answers at great length; he tries to explain why he seems to have betrayed them by his obscure speech and by the aloofness of his life. In the knowledge of his mission, a mission that is bound to separate him

47

from his fellows, the poet prays that he may not forget the memory of his fellow-men. Among them he is an exile, hardly recognizable by them, a sower of solitude, spreading anguish and distress.

Faites que je sois entre les hommes comme une
   personne sans visage et ma
Parole sur eux sans aucun son comme un sermon
   de silence . . .
Faites que je sois comme un semeur de solitude et
   que celui qui entende ma parole
Rentre chez lui inquiet et lourd.

The poet's 'marriage' has shut him off from the world. But marriage is a symbol of the indissoluble union of a soul with Christ. When the poet turns towards God, he possesses, with God, the entire creation. The Word was the gift of God Himself to the world. The poet's word is another gift to the world, to all created things. The closed house (*la maison fermée*) is an image of the world. The four doors of the house are the four points of the compass and, at the same time, the four cardinal virtues: prudence, force, temperance, justice. The poet sings of each one of these as he had once sung of the nine inseparable sisters, the nine Muses of the inner life.

And now, at the end, in a concluding hymn, he addresses the new century which has just begun:

Salut, aurore de ce siècle qui commence!

He sees the Catholic Church as the house made for the prayer of men: Notre-Dame, Solesmes, Ligugé. All the living belong to the Church, as do all the dead. The living, taking communion, and the countless dead all press around the same centre. The last page of the *Cinq Grandes Odes* is the poet's prayer for the dead. It is his answer to the harsh words of stricture at the beginning of *La Maison Fermée*. The symbol of the 'closed house' has by now assumed its widest significance, including and uniting all three churches: the Church militant, the Church triumphant, and all the dead in Purgatory.

In his theoretical writings, as well as in his odes, Claudel expresses the belief that the poet speaks from the centre of creation. He cannot look at any part of it without finding God, either in His transcendental form or in His Incarnation. The earth the poet contemplates is covered with signs of the spirit, from the time of the first Pentecost to the most recent and most humble, such as the experience of an adolescent French poet who wrote, 'la vraie vie est absente'.

The odes are spiritual exercises. All their richness and complexity may be reduced to the two primal subjects of Claudel's contemplation: poetry and love. The poet finds his real voice when he speaks of his personal experience of love, which is his call to perfection. The gigantic drama of the entire universe is set into motion each time a single soul begins its cycle of acceptance of divine love and resistance to it. Claudel believes that divine love addresses itself not to the noblest faculty in man but to that centre of his personality where the body and the soul are most intimately united. When man accepts this love, he realizes it exists outside his own power, independent and seemingly fortuitous. Whenever he betrays it in his preoccupation with the trivialities of existence, it becomes the great disturbing element in the heart of his being.

The poetics of Claudel stress the analogy between the poem and the creation. According to St Thomas, the order of the universe was willed by God. He had the idea of universal order before the creation: hence the belief that every human being pre-existed in God. The poet invokes in *La Muse qui est la grâce* his eternal archetype:

O idée de moi-même qui étais avant moi!
O partie de moi-même qui es étrangère à tout
    lieu et ma ressemblance éternelle qui
Touches à certaines nuits
Mon cœur . . .

The creation is the poem conceived in the mind of God. It is a unique and limited universe, each part of which bears relationship to all other parts, in the same way that a poem must obey the law of unity. The goal, therefore, of each creature is to live for the glory and justification of God. This doctrine is given a particular place of importance in *L'Esprit et l'Eau*.

Où que je tourne la tête,
J'envisage l'immense octave de la Création! . . .
Je ne vous vois pas, mais je suis contenu avec les
    êtres qui vous voient.

And again in *La Maison Fermée*, whose very title
explains the finiteness of the world:

O cher univers entre mes mains connaissantes!
    O considération du monde parfait à qui rien ne
    peut être soustrait ou ajouté.

The poetic word, therefore, derives its greatest
dignity from its relationship to the divine Word.
The very impulse urging the poet to speak is
comparable to the Holy Spirit in its collaboration
with the Word as the creating force. The most
succinct statement Claudel has made about his
poetics is a line in the second version of the early
play, *La Ville*:

Toute parole est une explication de l'amour.

Its meaning is undoubtedly to be found in the
Summa of St Thomas, in passages suggesting the
analogy between the function of the Holy Spirit
in the creation and the artist's emotion which is
able to effect the transition from the conception
of a work of art to its final expression.

The poet follows the teaching of the philosopher in his belief concerning the theocentric
finality of the universe. The universe is as much
an organic whole as is the human body. Even

aspects far separated in time and space are yet related. The poet's task is precisely the discovery of the mysterious dependence of one thing on all things. Physical forces and human wills concur in the composition of what we call a 'moment'. A brilliant passage in the *Art Poétique* describes the action of a hand moving from one side to the other of a page of paper and writing hundreds of words which lend to one another their force and colour, in the same way that the great physical forces of the heavens inscribe their details on the face of the earth. This is the basis for Claudel's theory of birth and knowledge. 'Toute naissance est une connaissance', and of the perplexing simultaneity of things. The earth is related to the heavens as the body is related to the mind. All things are necessary to one another.

Claudel has called himself 'the inspector of creation'. He learned to spell out things, to combine one word with another. He listened to the speech of many races and to many theories of existence, and he condensed all these in one continuous text. The earth which the poet tried to see in its totality is only one part of a vaster system. Before the immensity of the world, Claudel feels nothing of Pascal's terror, but rather a triumphant exaltation.

III

The Dramatist

The most serious attacks on the writings of
Claudel have been concerned with his plays. Except for a few scattered performances, they received no attention from the Paris theatres until
the last thirteen years of the poet's life. *Le Soulier
de Satin* was memorably produced by Barrault at
the Comédie-Française during the Occupation.
Partage de Midi was first played in Paris in 1948.
At the time of the poet's death, in 1955, *L'Annonce faite à Marie* was revived in a new production at the Comédie-Française.

The Claudel dramas are unlike anything in the
tradition of the French theatre. They follow
none of the conventions of Racine's classical
tragedy, of Hugo's romantic drama, of Augier's
realism, of Villier's symbolism. The first impression they give is one of unreasonableness, of
chaos, and even of irreverence. Claudel's earliest
and most permanent trait, that of a rebel, marks
his plays. They were composed in isolation, far
from Paris, and in opposition to the taste of the
day. Claudel created a dramatic form which is
unique in French and which bears a somewhat
vague resemblance to the dramas of Shakespeare
and Lope de Vega rather than to the tragedies and

comedies of his own country, which adhere closely to the Aristotelian precepts and the classical models. Claudel's drama is not a combination of the comic and the tragic; it is a work of one piece and one texture. It is simultaneously dramatic speech and poetry.

His characters speak with the voices of real men and women who feel that humanity forms one body, in that each man is responsible at every moment of his existence for all other men. In each scene of his many plays we have the impression of having shown to us some aspect of that most difficult and mystical of all dogmas, the communion of saints. For Claudel the universe is *one* at every moment of every man's existence. Every story he undertakes to tell, he finds to be an anecdote or an element of the same drama of man which is continuously unfolding in the world. Claudel has spoken of the 'passion of the universe' which he feels, and of the exaltation he derives from contemplating the millions of things which exist at the same time. 'Que j'aime ce million de choses qui existent ensemble!'

The first version of his first play, *Tête d'Or*, was written in 1890. It is his only non-Christian play. (Not until Christmas 1890, four years after his conversion, did Claudel take communion at Notre-Dame and formally return to the Church.) Claudel always attached a great deal of importance to this play. Long after its composition, he called it the 'introduction to his work' and 'the drama of the possession of the earth'. In its theme, and even partially in its style, it is, of all works of Claudel, the closest to Rimbaud. Rimbaud died in the hospital at Marseille in October 1891, two years after the first version of *Tête d'Or* was completed. In 1893, Claudel began his own career of travel, and composed in China, in 1894, the second version of *Tête d'Or*. It is the drama of a man, an adventurer, who attempts to assert himself by the sole means of his own strength and intelligence. This early text shows the poet's effort to come to grips with an inspiration which springs from spiritual tumult. The play raises many of the persistent problems of man's fate, without, however, the problem of woman's love, which is to be central in the later plays.

At the beginning of the play, the hero, Simon Agnel, is burying the woman he has loved and whose body he has brought back to their native soil. There he recognizes the younger man, Cébès, who had loved the same woman. This first part of the drama is a lament over the grave, spoken by the adolescent Cébès and by Simon. In the second part of the drama, Simon becomes Tête d'Or, the conqueror. He conquers all of Europe as far as the Caucasus, where he meets defeat and death. Behind the obvious impulse in Tête d'Or to seize the earth lies the problem of love, which is to develop in the subsequent plays into Claudel's principal theme. The tragedy in *Tête d'Or* comes from the hero's belief that he can find salvation in himself. He did not listen to the deepest voice within himself at the moments of his harshest lessons: the death of his wife, the death of Cébès, and his own death. In *Vers d'Exil*, written a year after the second version of *Tête d'Or*, Claudel gives in a single line the clue to his dramatic purpose:

Quelqu'un qui soit en moi, plus moi-même que moi.

This is Claudel's version of Rimbaud's celebrated 'Je est un autre'. It is the dialogue between man and God, the struggle between submission and resistance which is to inspire some of the noblest and most dramatic passages in Claudel's plays.

La Ville, Claudel's second play, written in 1890 and considerably revised in 1897, has as its theme the meaning of man's social existence. Besme is head of the city, the owner of the gardens and an engineer. His brother Lambert is not-too-successful a politician who, despite his age, wishes to marry a young girl, Lâla. Avare is the spirit of violence and destruction in the city. He recalls the character Simon in *Tête d'Or*. Cœuvre is the poet of the city. His scene with Besme, at the beginning of the play, is a dialogue between two opposing temperaments: between the poet, the isolated, excommunicated member of the group, and the leader who has discovered the vanity of all things. Lâla turns towards Cœuvre, and their marriage marks the end of the first act. This is the moment at which Lambert accepts the idea of his death, his brother Besme gives himself over to total despair, and the revolutionary Avare prepares the destruction of the city.

The one woman in the play, Lâla, dominates the second act. She is now living with Avare, the spirit of the future, having abandoned Cœuvre, the poet, who, as all poets, represents the present. When the city is in ruins—it is the setting of the third act—Avare leaves, because his mission is over. Ivors, the son of Lâla and Cœuvre, is lieutenant and in charge of the organization of a new city. Cœuvre himself returns to it in his new role of bishop. His life continues to be a search, but he speaks with authority about the constitution of the city, about the need to organize it as if it were a single body, with every member, from the prince to the lowliest contemplative, playing his part in the whole. Lâla is the first of Claudel's characteristic heroines: remote, mysterious, unknowable, a fascination interfering between man and God. From *Tête d'Or*, the study of a man alone with his powers, to *La Ville*, there has been a marked progress in Claudel's religious understanding of the world. After the study of man by himself, in his role of conqueror, Claudel now chose for the object of his contemplation the problems of a city.

By the time of the second draft of *La Ville*, 1897, all of Claudel's principal themes were present in his writings. Between the first and the second draft, the role of the poet Cœuvre, especially, was enlarged, and his allusions to the theory of his art were developed. The writing of the 1897 version coincided almost exactly with Claudel's study of St Thomas Aquinas. Abbé Friche has explored in his *Etudes Claudéliennes* the theory that Claudel grew more fully aware of his æsthetics thanks to his study of the philosopher. Claudel, the intuitive poet, found his justification in the metaphysical structure of the universe in accord with Thomistic thought. Symbolism, as defined by Mallarmé in his poems and in his theoretical writings, and by Rimbaud in *Lettre du Voyant*, is given a theocentric character in Claudel. The image of God which the poet offers in his work is the combined pictures of himself, in his deepest individuality, and of the world which he sees. In explaining the relationship of the poem to the poet, Claudel at the same time explains the relationship of the world to God.

The poet Cœuvre, on opening his eyes, feels himself the mirror of the world and longs to know his vision.

Et comme un miroir d'or pur qui renvoie l'image
    du feu tout entier qui le frappe,
Je brûlai d'un désir égal à ma vision, et tirant
    vers le principe et la cause, je voulus voir et
    avoir!

The analogy between the poet and God is completed when Claudel points out that the world was created by God, in an act of love, that of the Holy Spirit, and the poem is created by the poet, in an act of love for his Creator. 'Toute parole est une explication de l'amour' (*La Ville*). The

hidden symbolism of things and beings is revealed by the poet, and the means by which he
reaches this knowledge is not logic and reason
but contemplation. Cœuvre defines for Besme
the poet's act of contemplation:

O Besme, pour comprendre ce que je sais et ce
    que je dis,
Il t'est besoin d'une autre science,
Et, pour l'acquérir, oubliant un raisonnement
    profane, il te suffit d'ouvrir les yeux à ce qui
    est.

The lyric and dramatic poetry of Claudel does not
unfold in accord with logical thought, but in a
succession of scenes. Each element of these
scenes, which are both psychological and exterior,
is unknowable and inexplicable because it is part
of the totality of the universe and can never be
defined by a single man's limited knowledge and
experience.

In all the many versions he has written of his
best-known play, L'Annonce faite à Marie (first
called La Jeune Fille Violaine), Claudel stresses the
mystical paradox of human relationships. This is
particularly clear in the prologue, in the scene between the young girl Violaine and Pierre de
Craon, the builder of cathedrals. The bonds uniting these two are as mysterious and as strong as
those uniting Prouhèze and Rodrique in Le
Soulier de Satin. Pierre loves Violaine, and yet she
represents for him everything he is called upon
to give up: woman, happiness, the world itself.

His love scene is actually his scene of farewell to the world. The opening dialogue contains the whole meaning of the text and what lies beyond the text, because it analyzes the secret role which every Christian is called upon to play in the world. It is the role of pilgrim, the one who accepts the idea of separation. A kiss usually binds two lovers, but the kiss which Pierre gives to Violaine at the end of their scene is the sign of their separation. He has guessed the real meaning of her vocation. She is the victim who combines heroism with humility. Her example is the moral lesson of the play, and indeed of all of Claudel's plays. Pierre, as mason, architect, and builder of churches, just as every other character in the play, discovers his vocation upon earth. Violaine stands apart from them all, in that she is a symbol of eternity within time, of spirit within matter. Her vocation in the play itself adds a further dimension to the characters around her. By her very existence she reveals the meaning of the existence of those close to her: her father and her mother, her sister, her fiancé, and Pierre de Craon.

Violaine is the type of mystic who represents for Claudel an analogue with the poet. Although the goals of mystic and poet are different, many of their activities and disciplines bear striking resemblances. For certain degrees of knowledge the poet has to reach a deep inner silence, a spiritual freedom that amounts to complete detachment from the world. This stage precedes the real function of the poet who is by definition the maker of something. He is creator not in the sense that God is, who is able to create out of nothing. The poet is creator out of what the world provides. Claudel, coming after Baudelaire's important lesson on 'correspondences', has stressed this need of a collaboration between the artist and the world. A poem begins when a relationship is perceived.

At its inception, *L'Annonce faite à Marie* resembles a folk-tale or a village story. With a conventional plot, centering on two sisters, one good and one bad, Claudel yet achieved one of the noblest examples of poetic drama in French literature. The younger girl, Mara (whose name in Hebrew means 'bitter'), is envious of her sister Violaine. Like Cain and Abel, they come from the same origins and yet grow into two opposing forces. Mara's passion is for material things of the earth: the farm of Combernon and her inheritance. The role of Pierre de Craon grows in importance with each new version of the play. He is the stranger, the 'guest' who has no home of his own. The kiss which Violaine gives him at dawn will be sufficient to make impossible her marriage with Jacques Hury. Pierre is a leper, and Violaine in turn succumbs to the disease through her act of charity and love. Pierre, in a sense, is the image of the suffering king, Amfortas, the sinner, whose recovery is necessary for the health of all the inhabitants. He is a builder of churches in Claudel's own province, which is rich in masterpieces of the Gothic period: Reims, Soissons, Laon. The period of the play is the time of Jeanne d'Arc, the end of the Middle Ages and of the One Hundred Years War, a period of great distress for France, when the concepts of nation and national pride were beginning to emerge.

The second act, dominated by the scene between Violaine and Jacques, her fiancé, has the character of a consecration. Violaine is the victim reserved for a holy purpose: *Ecce ancilla Domini*. She has prepared herself for the sacrifice, and is even wearing the sacerdotal habit of the religious in the convent of Montsanvierge. She tries to explain to her fiancé why she cannot marry him. Her family is to end with her. As the Virgin is the last of the tree of Jesse, so Violaine is the last of the Vercors. Her relationship with Montsanvierge is as close as that uniting Mara with Combernon. The entire play is based upon an intimate relationship between nature and grace. Violaine's mystical vocation, which had been guessed and accepted by Pierre in the prologue, is not understood at first by Jacques.

In the third act the miracle happens. Violaine, the leper, is ostracized and about to die. Mara's baby daughter has died, and she approaches her sister as a last hope for resurrecting the child. The dialogue between the two sisters recalls in its profundity that between Ismene and Antigone. Life returns to the baby at the moment of the first Christmas mass. *Puer natus est nobis*. The epilogue is the awakening of Jacques. He realizes at last the innocence of Violaine and the evil of Mara. He knows, with the example of Violaine's death before him, that love is only in giving ourselves, in the power to give what we do not know. This truth, hard and harsh in purely human terms, is the centre of all the plays of Claudel. The sorrow of human love comes from its desire for complete possession; yet the soul, whatever its apparently rightful claims, cannot possess anything or anyone. Love has nothing to do with justice. These were the words spoken by Violaine in her renunciation scene of the second act.

The première of *Partage de Midi* took place on December 16, 1948, in Paris, at the Théâtre Marigny, exactly forty-two years after the play was written. In 1906, one hundred and fifty copies of the play had been privately printed. But further publication had been withheld by Claudel until 1948, when he re-issued the text and gave permission for its performance. Ten years previously, Jean-Louis Barrault had asked Claudel for the right to put on *Partage de Midi*. The poet had refused, saying at the time, 'You will play it after my death.' During the Occupation, Barrault's production at the Comédie-Française of *Le Soulier de Satin* was a triumph, and Claudel finally consented to a production of his older play, *Partage de Midi*, perhaps because he felt himself so far removed from the younger man who had written it. He was present at the rehearsals and introduced many changes in the text. But in directing and advising the actors he would refer to 'the author of the play', as though it had been written by a third person. It is a well-known fact that the play is the literary expression of an episode in Claudel's personal life.

Partage de Midi occupies a peculiarly central position in the entire work of Claudel. The drama concerns only four characters. Their speeches are long, sober, and bare. Each scene resembles a musical composition of two or three voices which reproduce a great variety of moods and tempi. The language controls and dominates all the movement, as if the actors had only to understand and recite it in order to discover the actions and the moods of the characters. The play remains at all times a majestic verbal quartet, each *motif* of which is persistent and in harmony with all other *motifs*. The principal theme is adultery, and the secondary theme is the struggle in a man between a religious vocation and sexual love. Ysé, the heroine, seeks in the three men around her, her husband and two lovers, an assurance or a stability which no one can give her and which she will find only in death. She is the dominant character of the play; it is around her that its principal theme is played out, a theme defined in Claudel's own terms, as 'the spirit desiring against the flesh' ('l'esprit désire contre la chair'). At the beginning of the play she is a coquette, provocative and seductive. But soon she reveals herself also as something of the bourgeoise, made for marriage and children, bent upon winning for herself material and emotional security. But fundamentally she is a biological force, opposing relentlessly the power of the spirit and manifesting for Claudel, the religious poet, the mystery of a creature's imperfection. Her femininity desires to reach and enfold everyone, and those whom she cannot conquer she will degrade.

Mesa, the leading male character, is the one whom Ysé desires the most and who is for her the most inaccessible. He is not only the lover who comes to a woman for the first time, but also that secret force in a man which is eternally unwilling to yield to human love. The religious idea of *Partage de Midi* might well be the impossibility of perfect human love, coming from the fact that we are beings separated from one another. The particular anguish expressed so abundantly in the love scenes between Ysé and Mesa comes from the desire, persisting even in possession, of a spiritual union, of a joining with the absolute.

In his own comments on *Partage de Midi*, Claudel dealt at some length with the character of Mesa, who at the beginning of the play, at the noon (*midi*) of his life, at the close of his youth, is returning to China after a vain effort to win a religious vocation. Then he is a bourgeois in the narrowest and meanest sense (Ysé calls him 'un sacré petit bourgeois'), totally preoccupied with himself. On the boat he meets the woman who is to teach him to prefer someone else to himself, and, eventually and mysteriously, God to himself. But the play is more subtle than Claudel's interpretation of it, which would seem to turn God into a magician and men into beings resembling puppets. Ysé is the central character, one of the most complex in the French theatre. Amalric, her first lover, sees her not as a coquette but as a warrior, as a conqueror, who wants to subjugate and tyrannize, or else give herself like some huge animal in pain. He feels that she is a stranger among men, separated from her land and race, looking for some tremendous duties and obligations. She seems incomparably stronger than Mesa, loving in absolute solitude a ghost and making him the passive partner in a tragedy entirely her own. For at the beginning of the play Mesa appears as a character incapable of any struggle, a conquest even before he is conquered. Ysé wages a combat with someone who does not fight.

The atmosphere of an ocean desert, evoked in the first act and pervading the whole play, envelopes Ysé's life. Claudel has provided for the stage version of his text a background explanation for the desert theme. When Ysé and her husband, de Ciz, appear in the first act, she states that they have been living in Harrar, where de Ciz in his trade of gun-runner was an associate of a certain Rimbaud, a man who paid no attention to her. Abandoning her husband, she turns towards the other two men. Mesa, the Christian, attracts her because he seems to offer the 'absolute' in love. Amalric fascinates her because of his strength, energy, and purposefulness. Together the characters, Ysé, her husband, and her lovers, form a quartet of guilty people. The action of the play takes place between the moment of noon (*partage de midi*), when each character makes a decision separating himself from his previous life, and the moment of midnight (*partage de minuit*), when the tragedy occurs, and death—a death of violence and sacrifice—joins Ysé and Mesa.

Partage de Midi demonstrates Claudel's growing power as dramatist and thinker. 'L'âme outrée, sortie de ton corps comme une épée, à demi dégaînée'—this is the main theme of the drama. Physical love is the anguish of a desire that transcends all possibilities of possession. One thinks of Phèdre, who, in Racine's tragedy, desires far more than the possession of Hippolyte. She yearns for that purity of which he is the physical image. But Ysé's great sin, greater than adultery, lies in her will to debase what she cannot possess.

Partage de Midi is, of all the plays of Claudel, the closest to pure tragedy. There is no supernatural intervention; and although the religious theme of human freedom and responsibility against the background of eternity is never lost sight of in all the complications of psychology, it is consistently enacted 'here and now'. Claudel has succeeded in raising the familiar and almost trivial story of adventure, violence, and adultery to the level of great religious drama without ever applying the lever of religious rhetoric. The force above these lives is either solar (*partage de midi*) or astral (*partage de minuit*), moving them towards a world which is the consummation of their world.

Claudel's greatest drama, *Le Soulier de Satin*, is at once one of the most complicated and one of the simplest plays ever written. The three principal characters enact a familiar plot: an aged husband, a young wife, and a lover. Yet from the personal relationships of these three characters there emerges the historical drama of the Renaissance. Even if dates and events are deliberately juggled with, one has the impression of watching the birth of a new era, of seeing a new world emerge from the mediæval world of St Thomas. Rodrigue and Don Camille are the types of conqueror and adventurer peculiar to that period. Their quest in all its worldliness is yet of a deeply spiritual nature. An obvious bond joins them with more modern adventurers, such as Rimbaud and T. E. Lawrence, and with travellers such as Paul Claudel himself.

In the Claudelian conception of drama, the relationship between man and woman, and between man and God, is an eternal relationship. If salvation is the goal of each human existence, love is the means for reaching this goal. Lovers in Claudel's plays appear as potential mystics. In *Le Soulier de Satin* and *Partage de Midi* he presents cases of human love so total that they would seem to exclude love of God, but Claudel, believing in the identity of all love, shows how erotic passion, as it grows in intensity, must end by recognizing the impossibility of its realization in purely human terms.

The questions about the destiny of passion, asked in such works as *Tristan*, *Phèdre*, *Manon*, are reiterated by Claudel: the meaning of passion, the reason for human love, the reason for its particular force, its destructiveness, the Christian attitude towards it, its spiritual meaning. His two great love dramas are violent in terms of the mystery surrounding the problem. A single man is insufficient to himself. He lives by need and desire for a complement. All of life manifests itself to Claudel in accordance with the idea of need and exchange. A lion leaps upon his prey to devour it, as a leaf turns yellow in order to provide the proper colour for a red leaf beside it.

Elle jaunit pour fournir saintement à la feuille voisine qui est rouge l'accord de la note nécessaire. (*La Ville.*)

A battle between two warriors is analogous to an exchange between two merchants. Innumerable relationships exist between the physical world and the world of men. The poet is the most apt to discover the mysterious complicity between things, and the immutable mystery of man in the change of civilizations.

Claudel calls woman, in *Partage de Midi*, the promise which cannot be held. ('La femme est la promesse qui ne peut être tenue.') She is not, like man's desire, infinite. The need for the infinite, which is at the basis of human love, is always deceived by love's limitations. It must be remembered that Claudel is not speaking of conjugal love in either play. He is quite literally and with unusual boldness studying the kind of passion treated previously in *Tristan*, *Phèdre*, and *Manon Lescaut*.

Claudel spent the five years between 1919 and 1924 in composing *Le Soulier de Satin*. He was living in Japan during most of this time. The earthquake in Tokyo occurred when he was there, and he lost part of the manuscript. The first performance took place, twenty years later, during the German Occupation of Paris, on November 27, 1943, at the Comédie-Française. For this performance Claudel rewrote the play, producing a considerably shortened version. It was staged by Jean-Louis Barrault, who also played the part of Rodrigue. The music was composed by Arthur Honegger.

The hero of the drama, Rodrigue, resembles the character of Tête d'Or, and the situation in which he finds himself is comparable to that of *Partage de Midi*. Claudel places his drama in the sixteenth century, which, contrary to the opinion of most historians, he sees as a period in which Catholicism was triumphant. He considers it the century of apostolic fervour, of the conquest of heresy, of the discovery of Plato and Greece, and of Divine Love manifesting itself in the experiences of St Teresa of Avila and St John of the Cross. The voyages of Vasco da Gama, Columbus, Magellan parallel the foundation of religious orders.

The action of the play covers an entire century. There is mention of the Council of Trent, held in 1545, and the paintings of Rubens, who died in 1640. Claudel freed himself from all the rules of unity. The universe becomes the scene of the action. The hemispheres carry on a dialogue with one another. In one scene, of great mystical importance, the earth itself takes on the size of a rosary bead.

In a prefatory note to *Le Soulier*, Claudel imagines his play performed before a large public on Mardi-Gras. The intention is clear: to shock and upset men in the midst of their festivities and pleasures, with the announcement of a religious truth. The prologue shows a victim attached to the mast of a sinking ship. He is a man of God, a missionary who speaks first of the tragic story of Rodrigue and prays for the salvation of his brother's soul. The force of this first character, who appears only in the prologue, is felt throughout the play. The action is built upon a constant intervention of Providence in the plans of man. Peace enters the heart of the priest at the moment of his sacrifice. Hope is the theme which will be elaborated throughout the long play, but it is fully present in the prologue, in the tortured position of the Jesuit priest. On the horizons around him lie continents which will be reconciled one with the other. Above him are the constellations of the heavens, and under him are the depths of the ocean. His soul is the entire Christian universe filled with the Presence.

As in *Partage de Midi*, two men are rivals for the love of a woman, Dona Prouhèze. (This name, Claudel confided to Louis Gillet, was discovered by him on a shoe-maker's sign in the rue Cassette, in Paris.) The experience of love makes the lover into a plaything of the Almighty, because love, being the source of grace as well as bearing an obscure relationship with sin, is the sign by which we are chosen. Dona Prouhèze's first marriage to Don Pélage, a worthy judge and adoring husband, meant a life of peace and inactivity, a life for which she was not made. She is a woman of action, who lives the most intensely in the presence of danger. At Mogador she falls in love with Rodrigue. She knows that this love is absolute and for all time. On the point of leaving Spain, she prays before a statue of the Virgin and places in the hand of the figure one of her satin slippers, so that when she rushes towards evil, she will go limping.

Je vous préviens que tout à l'heure je ne vous verrai plus et que je vais tout mettre en œuvre contre vous.
Mais quand j'essayerai de m'élancer vers le mal, que ce soit avec un pied boiteux!

Such an episode as this would have furnished the subject matter for a miracle play in the fifteenth century. Here it is the beginning of the drama between Rodrigue and Prouhèze, which, with two or three secondary plots, fills the 'four days' or the four long acts of *Le Soulier de Satin*, for which Claudel uses a vast range of characters.

Although it is a play on the subject of love, there is no love scene in the usual sense. The playwright separates his lovers, and keeps inventing ways to hold them apart. Only twice do they see one another, at the end of the second day and at the end of the third day. They are usually at opposite parts of the earth: Prouhèze, as governor of Mogador (in her husband's name), and Rodrigue, as viceroy of India. This story of love is a drama of absence, where each of the lovers accepts the fate of separation. This pain of separation, this wound in the souls of Prouhèze and Rodrigue, is precisely the place where God is at work.

Her guardian angel tells Prouhèze that it was God who created her love. Prouhèze had marvelled that God was not jealous of her love for Rodrigue, and the angel explains that even love in sin is able to serve God.

Dona Prouhèze.—L'homme entre les bras de la femme oublie Dieu.

L'Ange Gardien.—Est-ce l'oublier que d'être avec Lui? est-ce ailleurs qu'avec Lui d'être associé au mystère de Sa création?

Franchissant de nouveau pour un instant l'Eden par la porte de l'humiliation et de la mort?

73

D. P.—L'amour hors du sacrement n'est-il pas le péché?

A. G.—Même le péché! Le péché aussi sert.

This important scene between the angel and Prouhèze reveals the technique of salvation, which is the central theme throughout the long work. Grace works like a fisherman. Prouhèze is not only a capture for the angel, she serves also as a bait for Rodrigue.

In his preface, Claudel states that the play is the conclusion to *Partage de Midi*. Its realization is cast in a complex style, far more 'baroque' than any other work in the tradition of French lyrical drama. Henri Peyre says that 'it deserves better than any other literary work of recent times to be called baroque, if baroque means tension, a luxuriance of offshoots and an intricate blending of *genres*, nonchalant disregard of unities, acrobatic turbulence, lack of prosaic verisimilitude, and the whole world becoming a stage for a struggle towards divine love through human love'. A writer with fewer resources at his disposal would have exercised greater rigour and selective prudence, but to realize the enormous poetic vitality of Claudel means to accept the opulence of his language, his verbal incontinence, and his habit of recruiting dramatic characters among saints, angels, and stars.

The basic conflict in Claudel's dramas is found also in the plays of other contemporary dramatists: Giraudoux, Camus, Anouilh, Sartre. This conflict, whether it be within the individual himself, or between man and woman, or between an individual and society, is treated by Claudel with the specifically Christian emphasis on man's fate or rather on man's salvation. In the Christian sense, a hero accomplishes his highest destiny by establishing the right relationship with other creatures of God, by living with and for others. The spiritual and the carnal are two needs, two appetites, two realities. The usual conflict in a human being comes from the alternating force and seduction of these two poles. The spirit and the flesh each has its own truth. The Catholic dramatist recognizes these two contradictory truths and knows that only in their harmonization, in their unification, will salvation be realized.

Love, in its traditional literary treatment, is a study of passion, of the great force of attraction between man and woman, of the way in which two lives are changed by the violence and the rapture of this experience. Claudel deals dramatically with the metaphysical and theological aspects of his subjects. Woman, more than man, seems to be for him witness to the mystery of love which exceeds every lover. She aspires to a knowledge of the infinity of the experience which, in its more finite form, creates such suffering. Man, by contrast, remains closer to the earth, in his practical preoccupations, in his fidelity to needs and necessities. Rodrigue, for example, never forgets that he is the emissary of a king, both conqueror and ambassador. This difference in temperament between man and woman, which Claudel emphasizes accounts for the alternating wills to destroy and to worship. Above all, it announces the primitive unity, the intimate relationship between man and woman as they existed in God. The very pursuit of woman by man, in its ceaseless, unappeasable form, is sign of its high spiritual meaning.

In the two complementary dramas of Claudel, *Partage de Midi* and *Le Soulier de Satin*, the sacredness of love, which even in its most physical aspect tends towards the absolute, is represented together with the tragedy inherent in the lover's belief that the entire universe exists in the one loved. The most intense scenes in *Partage de Midi* re-enact the insatiable need for possession of the one loved and the exclusion of God from such an experience. When the lovers realize that they cannot suffice one another forever, the solitude they know then engenders death. The 'Cantique de Mesa' in the last act of *Partage* announces the story of *Le Soulier* and the solution reached by Rodrigue and Prouhèze in their Christian sacrifice of love. Claudel allots to woman the preeminent role in this process of purification. Her mission in the work of salvation is to incarnate divine tenderness and divine solicitude.

The conquest of the world and the tragedy of passionate love, two themes which are related, comprise the subject matter of *Le Soulier de Satin*.

The world is upset in its effort to reach a promised unity. Adventurers, merchants, kings, in their will to possess the earth and to unite the parts of the earth, provide the background for the human tragedy of Rodrigue and Prouhèze. Just a few episodes and a few moments prevent the total tragedy and announce the salvation: the slipper left with the statue of the Virgin, the angel watching over Prouhèze, St James and the other saints, the young daughter of Prouhèze. All the tumult and upheaval in the action of the long play fall into place when Rodrigue releases Prouhèze (at the end of the Third Day) and by this renunciation welcomes the peace of God and the silence which had been announced by the Jesuit priest in the prologue.

Between *Tête d'Or* of 1890 and *Le Soulier de Satin* of 1924, French poetry lived through a period rich with experimentation. From today's point of view Claudel's position is at the very head of the experiments with language which characterize symbolism and surrealism. In many ways, *Le Soulier* seems consecrated to the tenth muse, Grace, but it is also composed in a new understanding of poetic freedom. No one word can define it: poetry, prose, history, theology. It is all these combined.

Before its composition, during the years preceding the First World War, Claudel had reached a degree of glory—not celebrity—that was equivalent to the glory of two other figures of the same period, Bergson and Rodin. Then, after the war, Claudel lost favour with the literary world. The younger writers could not forgive him for being an 'official', a dignitary. The post-war excesses of artistic experimentation blinded them to the fact that Claudel too had always been essentially an experimentalist. The hostility against Wagner which this new generation felt was of the same kind as the hostility against Claudel. Apollinaire was the poet triumphant with the young. They formed a group around Picasso who supported the music of Satie and *les Six*. Only Darius Milhaud remained faithful to Claudel.

Claudel returned to favour at the end of the 'thirties. The many facets of his writing were discovered and rediscovered at this time, and by young and old alike. The moment was propitious for the première of *Le Soulier de Satin* in 1943, despite the tragedy of that year in France. The new readers found in Claudel an intellectual stimulant. The fact that he was not obscure in the surrealist manner was now felt to be an attraction, and it was seen that his apparent verbal mannerisms contained a greater degree of intelligibility than ordinary language. No doubt his new success was bound up with his presentation of a full physical sensual life, even of violence and brutality; and indeed he had profited from the achievements of the symbolists, from thirty years of poetic acrobatics in developing his own eloquence, with its remarkable suppleness, abundance, and weightiness. His full-blooded characters—Tête d'Or, Avare, Pierre de Craon, Amalric, Rodrigue—were men of flesh and spirit. Over and over again in these plays humanity was represented as one body for which each one of us is responsible at every moment of our lives.

Le Soulier de Satin is many things at once: the historical drama of the Renaissance when the great schism split asunder the Church and a new civilization was founded; a drama of action and adventure where strong men created new empires or wandered over the face of the earth to find a place with nothing in it to remind them of their native lands; a drama of human relationships existing despite long separation; a drama of love, finally, where love is never passivity or rhetorical effusion. Throughout his drama Claudel is saying that love of man for woman is love of an illusion, love of something which only seems to exist. The Romantics had preached that love is God; Claudel reverses this phrase in order to restate, through the example of his most passionately human characters, the Scriptural message that God is Love.

IV

The Apologist

Claudel was the last survivor of a group of writers who have made the year 1900 as significant in the history of French letters as the years 1660 and 1830. They were three moments when the genius of a few writers transformed the French language and offered a new picture of the world. Two of his peers, Valéry and Gide, died within the decade preceding his own death, and the third, Proust, died much earlier, in 1922. Several other writers can almost be placed in this foremost rank: Péguy, Apollinaire, Bergson, Colette. Success came slowest to the last survivor, to Claudel, who shows, as every greater writer does, the reflection of his century, but who also shows traits less temporal, more hidden, more resistant. It is possible, although it is too soon to know with any certainty, that those very traits of intractibility will assure Claudel's work a more enduring significance.

He was fully aware of the contradictions in his nature, and often acknowledged his faults, his egoism, his avarice, his bourgeois characteristics. He was struck by the fact that man learns of God's will only by contradicting it. And yet Claudel's particular power as a writer is a coincidence of opposites: the sensitivity of a poet and the hardness and shrewdness of a peasant; the attractions of the world and the quest for spiritual joy. Throughout his work, but especially in his correspondence with Gide, Claudel contrasts the Sage of antiquity with the Christian. Whereas the Ancient lived in a state of equilibrium and harmony, the Christian lives in a state of tension and conflict. Hence the office of the poet is not foreign to the office of the apologist. Both exist in order to awaken in mankind an awareness of a void and of a lack, a need for the presence of God.

At the end of his life, Claudel was hostile to Pascal, who is still the most celebrated French apologist. But at the time of his conversion he knew something of Pascal's *pleurs de joie* and Pascal's vocation for solitude. At the beginning, Claudel's ignorance of the history of the Church made it possible for him to minimize her role. This changed with time, and Claudel gradually grew into the Catholic apologist who looked upon his world as an assembly of false gods. His religious story had begun in Notre-Dame, as he listened to the singing of a Bible text, Mary's hymn of the *Magnificat*. His Bible studies often refer to the figure of Woman in the book of *Proverbs*, who symbolizes the Wisdom of God. It is always the same figure, whether he calls her Muse or Wisdom or Grace or Virgin or indeed the Church herself.

The letters exchanged between Gide and Claudel form the most recent dialogue between two opposing voices. Charles du Bos once called Montaigne and Pascal, the sceptic and the believer, the exemplary partners of 'the great French dialogue', a dialogue which he says every Frenchman conducts within himself. A dialogue such as that between Montaigne and Pascal, or between Bossuet and Fénelon, or between Gide and Claudel is a manifestation of the critical spirit. The Frenchman listening to it prefers not to take sides, and not to sacrifice one for the other.

Claudel, the man of serene faith, is opposed to Gide, the man of restless inquiry. On the one hand, we read an expression of exultant joy, of a vision of peace, held up before all men; and, on the other hand, we read the narrative of an endless search for happiness, sought in all forms of pleasure. The correspondence reveals the tremendous dialectical effort Claudel made, between 1900 and 1926, to convert Gide to Catholicism. Whereas the letters of Claudel show his complete thought on the subject discussed, those of Gide we have to read in conjunction with the entries in his *Journal*, written at the same time, in order to follow his mind accepting and rejecting almost simultaneously. Claudel is a vociferous catechizer, but his correspondent is reticent and cautious. This dialogue, which ended in 1926, is one of the most vehement and engrossing in the history of French literature. Although not many years have passed since it ended, it can be read now as the most recent example in France of Pascalian apologetics to which the contemporary

Montaigne replied with a seemingly definitive 'No'.

André Gide often gives the impression in his letters of playing hide-and-seek with Claudel; and yet his attitude cannot with justice be called hypocritical. If he could write as boldly and frankly as a Montaigne, he was quite timid in speech. The physical presence of Claudel inhibited him. After their meetings together, Gide would put down in his *Journal* the arguments he had not been able to articulate.

The Catholicism of Paul Claudel is commanding and imperial. He is a poet speaking with the force of lyricism. He communicates his enthusiasm. The answers of Gide have their own formal beauty, their own careful refinement. Even after Gide confessed the secret of his life, Claudel continued to exhort and preach. Whenever Claudel spoke from the viewpoint of dogma, there was almost no reaction from Gide. By nature, Gide could not be impressed with the scholastic concepts which form most of the intellectual argumentation of the poet. Claudel's temperament led him to describe the modern world as if he were a mediæval man enlightened by scholastic ontology. Gide's temperament was fundamentally suspicious of any such massive construction of the mind. Much of Gide's work, written after his debate with Claudel, was to represent a secularization of the Gospels.

During the last twenty years of his life Claudel did not publish poetry or plays. He spent his time writing his reflections and his meditations on Holy Scripture. These works form not only an epilogue to his long career as a poet and dramatist but a continuation of it. The active contemplation which was always an element in Claudel's earlier books simply became the exclusive element in his studies of the Bible.

He always claimed that Rimbaud had been one of the great explorers of the nineteenth century, consecrated to learning what the created world really is and signifies. The basis of symbolism is a belief that each thing in the world has a meaning which will be revealed to the poet who is able to understand his vocation. Claudel received this belief in the universal symbolism of the world almost as a mission. After learning how to read the universe, he learned how to read the poetry of the Bible in a similar method of deciphering. He brought to the words of the sacred writings the same devoted attention he once lavished on the material objects of his world. The poet of *Cinq Grandes Odes* and *Corona Benignitatis Anni Dei* became the fervent and meticulous reader of Isaiah and St John.

St Teresa, in her celebrated commentary on *The Song of Songs*, explains that she does not understand the mysteries of the poem but that those very mysteries give her delight. Claudel devoted two years of meditation to *The Song of Songs*, and his book, *Paul Claudel interroge le Cantique des Cantiques*, is a long study of it. Each verse of the Bible text is turned in all directions and analyzed

with consummate ingenuity. He does not claim
to have written the definitive exegesis of the
work, nor to offer a positive explanation. At the
beginning of his book, Claudel ridicules many of
the famous images in the poem, which he refuses
to consider a love-song. It is, for Claudel, an epith-
alamium, a song celebrating a mystical marriage.
Whatever the poet is doing or experiencing in
his daily life is absorbed by his interpretative
passion. The day after the première of *Le Soulier
de Satin*, in December 1943, Claudel returned to
Brangues and resumed the writing of his commentary. He writes at length of his own play,
which he considers a nuptial drama, just as he
considers the *Song of Songs* the poem of mystical
marriage. The book is rich in personal reminis-
cence: Paris about 1886, the consulate at Fou-
Tcheou, Renan, cathedrals, boats on the Pacific.
It is a somewhat extravagant book, but for those
who are receptive to the imaginative powers of
Claudel, it will remain a great record of devotion
and meditation.

Emmaüs is a book of three hundred pages, a
long meditation on the meeting of the two disciples with Jesus on the road to Emmaus. Claudel, whose own conversion had been unpre-
pared, speaks of the supremacy of grace, the
initiative which God takes. The study is replete
with allusions to contemporary life. Gide and
Proust are symbolized by the figure of Absalom,
caught in the tree by his hair. They are termed
'exhibitionists'. Claudel calls them champions of

'self-reliance', 'éternellement livrés à un balancement pendulaire entre le Oui et le Non. Ils pendent.' History and symbolism, in all of his books of scriptural exegesis, are fused and the one explained by the other. Claudel sees, for example, in the sacrifice of Abel the prefiguration of the Mass. He goes so far as to say that the Holy Spirit is not only the author of the Bible, but the author of the history of the Church as well.

In a letter from Washington, April 21, 1932, Claudel had written that henceforth he was done with literature in the usual sense and would devote his writing to meditations on the Bible. His contributions to this study have revived the old disputes between symbolists and historians, between theological and literal exegetes. In St Luke's narration of the episode of Emmaus he tells how Christ, before revealing Himself to the two disciples, reminded them of all the events which had announced his coming. Claudel, likewise, returns to the Old Testament to describe the various symbols of the Father of whom the Son was later to speak. He exploits all the subtle and learned art of symbolism. In this kind of study there is always the danger of accumulating too many layers of meaning for any one object or any one event, and indeed, Claudel's very virtuosity is at times difficult to follow.

A recent book of his, *Paul Claudel interroge l'Apocalypse*, is a clear demonstration of his method and his belief in symbolism as the key to our knowledge concerning Divine Truth. This work is written in radical opposition to the literal or scientific exegesis of Holy Scripture. In his treatment of the symbols of St John, Claudel assumes the role of prophet and man of God whose mission is to speak in the name of God. Such an examination as Claudel undertakes is no mere game of erudition. His effort is vigorous, consecrated, and inspired. This book was composed during the darkest months of the last war. It was completed in December 1942. The temporal catastrophes were seen as related to the real Apocalypse, which for Claudel is a spectacular drama of all times in which we all have our parts. The *Revelation* of St John ceases to be the mysterious book of the Bible in the course of this interrogation of Claudel. He transposes it into a work of surprising reality. Never has the style of Claudel resembled so closely the polemical vituperations of Léon Bloy. He denounces the sterility of humanism, the scepticism of Renan, the Buddhist Nirvana in its denial of Being, the attempt of Protestantism to place God at the service of man. But such themes, and they are are abundant, are always subordinate to Claudel's very personal interpretation of the *Book of Reveltion*. He points out that Satan is called Lucifer (Lux) and that the apostasy of the West is called the Enlightenment. The Scarlet Woman is first the Paris of Claudel's youth, and then any great city of the modern world.

The seriousness of Claudel's religious sentiment dominates everything in his work. It lies at the source of each poem, play, and essay. Whether the subject is specifically religious or not, the tone and the lyricism are religious because, for Claudel, the poet is at all times the servant of truth. In a letter to Jacques Rivière, he claims that art is a pâle duplicate of holiness. ('L'art n'est qu'une pale contrefaçon de la sainteté.') Claudel is bent upon discovering the deepest meaning of his personal experiences, indeed of all of his varied dealings with the world. Religious art, in the narrowest sense, is concerned with the mysteries of religion, but in its broadest sense, with the mysteries of the world. For Claudel, the divine is constantly intervening in the life of man.

A meeting with the impressario Reinhardt in Washington, in 1927, led Claudel to study the character of Columbus. He wrote the play, *Le Livre de Christophe Colomb*, in Brangues, during the vacation months of that year. The music was composed by Darius Milhaud. The first production took place in Berlin, in 1930. In France, much later, in 1953, it was staged by Jean-Louis Barrault at the Marigny. The ultimate value of this text may well lie in Claudel's analysis of genius and in his—unmistakably autobiographical—treatment of certain traits in Columbus's character.

Jean Amrouche was the first to point out the resemblance between the historical 'discoverer' and the poet. Claudel studies Columbus as the genius in his relationship to tradition, and as the victim of his own greatness. The poet's imagination, in the circuit of its inner adventure, bears analogy with the exterior conquest of Columbus, who, before his triumph, knew defeat and humiliation. Each in his own way, Columbus and Claudel sought the reunion of the scattered parts of humanity. Christendom sprang up in the lands bordering the Mediterranean—Palestine, Rome, Greece, Gaul, Spain—and it spread to the world through the action of discoverers and apologists.

In their own way the arts have never ceased to proclaim immortality, and in a sense it is even true to say that their highest concern is to bestow everlasting life on our highest moments of perception. For apathy endangers the vitality of our perception and of every virtue we may possess. By creating works of art, man is able to endow his perceptions with a kind of immortality. Most of our perceptions pass by rapidly and disappear into a void. Our incapacity to hold them is cause for sorrow and melancholy. Art sets up the goal of preserving them.

Many of the most serious of twentieth-century artists have been concerned with providing their works with an æsthetic justification. In the field of painting, for example, Braque has made theoretical pronouncements of considerable importance. Others, while not contributing any writing as massive as Delacroix' *Journal*, have spoken at times with conviction and acumen: Picasso,

Matisse, Rouault, Masson, Severini. In literature, the particular achievement of Marcel Proust is the masterful way in which he combined in his novel artistic creation with an analysis of its origin and meaning. Joyce, Mann, Gide, Valéry were all engaged in producing works of art and, at the same time, the æsthetics of their works. In the same way, the first of the five great odes of Claudel is a kind of poetics dealing with the poetic act, with its birth and its function.

On many points the theories of Claudel coincide with those of Proust, and before him, with the tenets of impressionism and the theories of Ruskin. These artists and theorists believe that each time a new original artist arises, the world is re-created. He is able to confer immortality on what has no duration—on man's perception of the world. Æsthetic truth is not the same as scientific truth. It is not based on direct observation or exact notations. The reality of the world for an artist is his vision of the world. It is a particular universe not seen by other men until it is put in the form of art. The public is ignorant about art or indifferent to new artistic creations, but each work will create its own posterity, and will reveal to it the soul and the temper of the period in which it was created.

Things of the world cannot really be possessed save in the form of that eternity which art creates. In making his metaphors or in effecting his metamorphoses, the poet or painter brings about a purer and more intimate contact between man and his world. The modern artist, whether he be Claudel or Proust, Rouault or Picabia, is greatly concerned with the relation existing between creations of art and the reality of the world. Metaphor and metamorphosis are signs of the sovereign freedom of man's mind to transform what we usually call reality into meaningful manifestations of the spirit.

Life consists for us in a series of scenes and pictures. Most of them disappear and sink into oblivion. Our personality is constantly being formed by time and destroyed by time. The objective of art is the elucidation and eternalization of those elusive scenes. In the very act of creation the artist explores the meaning of those fleeting impressions and fugitive sensations. The difference between works of art does not lie so much in divergent techniques as in qualitatively varying visions of individual artists. Art alone is able to show us how the universe appears to someone else.

The problem of modern art, and especially the Christian idea of modern art, must needs be central to any study of the writings of Paul Claudel. No single figure, not even the painter Rouault, has called forth such contradictory judgments from his critics. Whichever view is held, whether Claudel is regarded as the greatest contemporary Catholic poet or seen as an example of the incommunicability of modern art, the claims inherent in such judgments are usually as big as are the dimensions of the work itself. Some of the more recent evaluations of Claudel have pointed out that the fate of his work, which suffered first from public indifference, and then from public hostility, and thirdly from a marked division of praise and blame, testifies to the present state of Christianity, which has lost its vitality and self-assurance.

It would be difficult to find another contemporary artist whose religious belief or æsthetic philosophy is as much the object of controversy as are the principles and forms of his art. Claudel has been attacked with equal strength on the score of his Catholicism and on the score of his art. Pierre Lasserre, one of the most vehement critics of the French poet, states that Claudel rejected the heritage of the Renaissance and embraced an archaic mediævalism. He thereby, according to Lasserre, repudiated all philosophical reflection and progress, and separated himself from the central tradition of French literature. Frédéric Lefèvre, one of the earliest ardent defenders of Claudel, claims, on the contrary, that the humanism of the Renaissance was reactionary, and Claudel's main glory is that of having resurrected mediæval humanism.

The controversy about Claudel, in which so often the very principles of modern art are the point at issue, is particularly significant when either side is represented by Catholic writers. Henri Massis, who follows strictly the theories of Pierre Lasserre, believes that the æsthetics of Claudel are not in agreement with the principles his art is trying to demonstrate. Massis finds in the subjective lyricism of Claudel an incommunicability and a disorderliness which are contrary to the spirit of order, discipline, and hierarchy inherent in the Revelation in which the poet believes. The original apostolic fervour is sacrificed, for Massis, to a certain esoteric and hermetic quality of his work. This attack is obviously levelled at the school of symbolism as well as at the specific art of Claudel. In order to get to the bottom of such a controversy, it would be necessary to consider the difficult and tortuous rhetoric of Claudel as the poet's means of conveying his vision of man, of this creature of contradictions, torn between the demands of the flesh and the spirit. The question then would be: is Claudel the modern poet who has achieved a synthesis of the æsthetics of Rimbaud and of the teachings of St Thomas Aquinas?

It is difficult to dissociate the work of a Christian poet, such as that of Claudel, from the teachings of the Church on art. These teachings, through the centuries, are not dogmatic as are the teachings on morals and theology. They emphasize different points in different periods because of the varying characteristics of art. But the great doctors of the Church and the mystics appear in agreement that there are, generally speaking, two ways to God.

The first is usually referred to as the 'way of signs'. Nature and all the myriad parts of the physical universe are, in this sense, signs. Our

sensibility might become so heightened and puri-
fied that our very sense-perceptions would be
religious experiences. The manifestations of art
are perhaps a further and more complicated development of this same communion, carried on
through the senses, between man and the world.
For art is the stylization, or the extension, of
nature by means of an emotion expressed significantly. Liturgical art differs from other forms of
art only in being dedicated to the highest of all
mysteries. For is not, according to Christian
dogma, God the Creator of the universe? If so,
then the world may be an instrument of sanctifica-
tion. The very nature of man, which moves from
the physical to the spiritual, parallels the nature
of the universe and its spiritualization in art.
Nature is as full of signs as is the Bible, and there
is no more a clear separation between the sensible
and the intelligible than there is between the body
and the soul. This 'way of signs' is based upon a
belief that God is immanent in His universe and
in His creatures. St Francis of Assisi expresses
this immanence of God in the poem usually
called *Canticle of All Creatures*, in which he addresses his brother the wind and his sister the
moon. Dante uses the figure of the beloved as
guide to the summit of Paradise—Beatrice, who
is the Christian counterpart of Diotima in Plato's
Symposium. Giotto's madonnas as well as Rouault's clowns and prostitutes illustrate the 'way
of signs' and the immanence of God in His
creation. Claudel stresses the importance of the

94

'immense octave of creation' in the drama of his conversion.

The other way to God leads beyond signs. In this far more ascetic way, Nature is avoided, art, and even liturgy, is rejected. The belief upon which this way is based is the transcendence of God. St John of the Cross is its great explorer. This second way, when it is really reached, lies beyond the first, but it is often lost sight of for its caricature: radical Jansenism, a pessimism such as Pascal experienced at times. Man is called upon to remain on the 'way of signs', where Nature, art, and liturgy may guide him, until he is able to move on to the second without being led astray by the un-Christian by-passes of the 'way beyond signs'.

In the course of the nineteenth century there grew up a particular 'bourgeois' form of Catholicism. It was a Catholicism far more moralistic than spiritual, far more Jansenistic than purely Christian. It must be remembered that the Jansenistic spirit is on the whole hostile to art. The ideal of the bourgeois Christian was an ideal of personal perfection, of personal success, rather than a love of God and the sensible world. During the first fifty years of the twentieth century, some of the leading Catholic writers, such as Bloy, Péguy, Bernanos, Mauriac, have attacked, in their novels and polemical writings, the ideals of the Catholic bourgeoisie. It may become obvious in time that they were engaged in a profound and, as things were, revolutionary re-assertion of Christian values, a movement to which the achievements of a poet like Claudel and a painter like Rouault significantly contribute. Claudel's closeness to his peasant ancestry and his imperviousness to any Jansenistic influence help to explain the quality of joyous praise pervading his entire work, and the precedence which in him the spiritual takes over the moral. He calls himself a 'rassembleur de la terre de Dieu', and the earth he calls a text which teaches jubilation.

Both the Catholic writer emphasizing a polemical message, in the manner of Péguy and Bernanos, and the Catholic artist of the type of Claudel and Rouault show the strong desire to illuminate for the contemporary world the mystery of that dogma which is primarily concerned with joy: the mystery of the communion of saints, with its universal solidarity of all the souls who have been born and who will be born. In this mystery, suffering and evil are given a mystical meaning by the supernatural hope which infuses the world with the promise that one day the memory of sin will be effaced. Claudel sees history in the image of a single unbroken sentence unfolding throughout time until it reaches its finally revelatory and finally triumphant clause.

Claudel's parable on Animus and Anima may well have been written to explain the principle of analogy. It is about the marriage of mind and soul. Animus is the part of us which divides and separates and analyzes. Anima is the part which unites and makes us one. The parable of Animus and Anima is Claudel's version of the struggle of opposites within existence, a struggle which has been interpreted in some form or other in every period of history and by every major thinker. Father D'Arcy, in *The Heart and Mind of Love*, uses Animus and Anima to explain Eros and Agape. The terms correspond to many pairs of opposites, both general and specific: male and female, romantic and classical, life and death, egoism and self-sacrifice, the conscious and the unconscious, Dionysus and Apollo.

This celebrated pair, Animus and Anima, or Eros and Agape, appear under countless names. Jungian psycho-analysis defines anima as the centre of the irrational and the unconscious, the abode of the dark passions and instincts, the archetype of both aggressive and seductive forces. Anima, thus defined, can easily be recognized as the persistent Muse of Romanticism. On a higher level, however, that is, on the level of Claudel's parable and of Henri Bremond's *Prière et Poésie*, anima seems to signify poetic or mystical knowledge. Animus is the surface self—'le moi de surface, le *je* qui s'agite à la circonférence de l'âme'. Anima is the deep self—'le moi profond, qui s'unit aux réalités, qui reçoit les visites de Dieu'.

In this parable of the two selves, or the two parts of the soul, it is obvious that harmony is not easily achieved between *animus* and *anima*. The temptation of animus is the love of self, which may weaken the love of God; and the temptation of anima is, in the romantic sense, the excessive emancipation of the deep self and the resulting contempt of reason. Only in their ideal marriage is true humanity realized.

Claudel's Catholicism has the impassioned fullness and vitality we associate with the Middle Ages, which had to a large extent disappeared in Europe with the early Renaissance. The *Odes* of Claudel express the spirit's joy and sorrow, exaltation and anguish in the contemplation of the world, a concrete spirituality which has its counterpart in the French Gothic cathedrals. When Christendom moved beyond its moral and theological systems assuming concrete shape in stone and mortar, the whole world with its animals and saints, rogues and birds, trees and berries, roots, branches, and leaves was assembled in, on, and around buildings large enough to house all the inhabitants of the city on market days, feast days, and days of penance. The cathedral invoked all the realms of Nature to give witness to the reality of the supernatural.

The appearance of Claudel's poetry in the twentieth century is not unlike the appearance of the Gothic cathedral in the thirteenth. They are comparable in their depiction of the every-dying and ever-reborn forms of the world. In them, symbolism and theology are bound up with life. The mediocre types of churches which have been built during the past century and a half testify to the spiritual impoverishment of modern humanity. The poetry of Claudel is a reminder that artistic creation is concerned with human realities, and that sacred art, if it is unable to attain to the market-place concreteness of architecture, may yet reach new heights in writers who, paradoxically, are not always fully accepted by the Church, such as Bernanos and Claudel, and in painters, such as Rouault and Matisse.

Perhaps the greatest lesson that Claudel has to teach is that the true 'realism' of art always tends towards the sacred. To the extent to which this truth is increasingly realized, we may be justified in speaking of a renascence of sacred art. The chapel of Matisse at Vence, in Southern France, illustrates this contemporary hope. The conversation between the aged bishop of Nice and the aged painter (who was not a practising Catholic) revealed a remarkable similarity of spiritual life in the priest and the creative artist, a revelation which may have taken both by surprise.

The sanctuaries recently erected at Assy, Audincourt, and Vence appear as original and new as the odes of Claudel did when they were first published; as new and original, too, as the clowns and Christs in the paintings of Rouault. These particular examples of Christian art have met with the same criticism as modern art in general; men of the Church have called them subversive and perverse. Nevertheless, compared to religious works of the nineteenth century, they show a significant change. The nineteenth century has no religious artist of the stature of either Claudel or Rouault. If the Church has only a little more use for Rouault, Matisse, or Claudel than it had for Delacroix, Cézanne, or Rimbaud, the fact remains that, while the latter had no use for the Church either, this is indeed not true of Claudel and Rouault.

The uncertainty of the Church is not surprising, for there is no one authoritative Christian treatise on æsthetics. In the twentieth century, men like Thomas Gilby and Jacques Maritain have tried to cull from the voluminous writings of St Thomas Aquinas a sufficient number of precepts which might form the basis of such a treatise. The *Art Poétique* of Claudel, and all of his writings, for that matter, substantiate and illustrate what perhaps can be called Aquinian æsthetics.

For the Thomist, the problem of the æsthetic revolves around our knowledge of the concrete. The concrete is the field of experience, the centre of poetic knowledge, as opposed to rational knowledge, which is always general, abstract, and conceptual. Our deepest desire is to know the real, and in this sense, æsthetic experience may be the satisfaction in us of a persistent craving. The world itself, in its immediate reality, provided Claudel with an inexhaustible supply of impressions, pictures, customs, colours, and words. He is the type of universal artist interested in every culture, every mythology, every landscape. All instances of human life and activity, all aspects of Nature, all laws and all forms of knowledge are of interest to the poet. But the only material the poet uses is words, and it is for words that Claudel claims a secret virtue which the poet alone is able to use to the full. The word, as it is used by the poet, is not the conventional sign that it is in prose and ordinary speech. It is more like a magic formula, an incantation capable of calling forth the true nature of the thing for which the word stands. The poet's words, for Claudel, create and re-create the primitive reality of the world.

The poet's art reflects, therefore, the fundamental nature of the world. At each moment in time the world is renewed. The artist, in producing his works, perceives more clearly than anyone else this principle of perpetual change and renewal of the world. If Thomistic doctrine holds that our deepest desire is to *know* the real, it also says that a thing may be more *loved* than it is known. St Thomas believed that, although we can love God perfectly, we know Him imperfectly. The relationship of love to knowledge is the central problem in Thomistic philosophy as well as in Claudel's æsthetics. If only God's will, which is love, can give existence to concrete things, then they can only be truly known through love; and this is the artist's mode of knowledge.

The relationship of the poet to his poem is comparable to the relationship of God to His universe. In Claudel's æsthetics the universe is seen as the mirror of God, and man as the mirror of the universe. It is through the arrangement of words that the poet mirrors the world. Thus the knowledge that a poem contains cannot be abstracted from the poem's concrete and total reality. It *is*, in fact, the poem's concrete reality. Here the parable of Animus and Anima seems to apply to the poet's re-creation of the world. The surface self, the animus, is constantly composing words into clear, simple, intelligible notions. But these are not the words of the poet. The poet's words are prompted by anima, rising from the inmost core of his being. They are obscure to the poet himself until they have passed through the ordering but gentle fingers of animus, retaining even then, and then still more clearly, the integrity of their origin.

APPENDIX

Translation of French passages in the text

p. 26.   For when you speak, as a tree through all its leaves moves in noonday silence, peace gradually in us absorbs our thought.

You explain nothing, O poet, but all things through you become clear to us.

p. 32.   O grammarian in my verse! Do not look for the way, look for the centre!

p. 36.   But you put me on the earth, for me to endure pain and awkwardness and obscurity,
And the violence of the other stones pressing against me,
And for me to occupy my place, forever like a cut stone which has its form and weight.

p. 36.   See that I, who do eternal things with my voice, be wholly
That voice, a fully intelligible word!

p. 40.   O my soul! the poem is not made from these letters I plant like nails but from the white which remains on the paper.

p. 42.   Thus when you speak, O poet, in a loving enumeration
Uttering the name of each thing,

Like a father you call it mysteriously by its principle, and as once
You participated in its creation, you co-operate in its existence!
Each word a repetition.

Do you not feel my hand on your hand?
(And in truth, I felt, I felt her hand on my hand!)

p. 43. Lord, my being longs for you!
Free me from myself! Free my being from itself!
I am free, deliver me from freedom!

p. 44. You are visible in this world as in the other.
You are here I can be nowhere save with you.

p. 46. Leave me alone! Let me do as I wish.

I will sing the great poem of man removed from chance!

p. 48. Grant me to be in the midst of other men a person without a face and my
Word be on them without sound like a sermon of silence . . .
Grant me to be a sower of solitude and grant that he who hears my word
Will go home worried and distressed.

Hail, dawn of this new century!

p. 50.   Idea of myself who was before me!
          Part of myself who is a stranger in every
place, and my eternal resemblance which
          Touches on certain nights
          My heart . . .

p. 51.   Wherever I turn my head,
          I behold the tremendous octave of Creation!
          . . .

          I do not see you, but I am encompassed by
the beings who see you.

          Beloved universe in my knowing hands!
          Thought of the perfect world from which
nothing can be subtracted and to which
nothing can be added.

p. 58.   And like a mirror of pure gold reflecting
the image of the whole fire which strikes it,
          I burned with a desire equal to my vision,
and moving toward the principle and the
cause, I wanted to see and to have!

p. 59.   O Besme, to understand what I know and
what I say,
          You need another science,
          And to acquire it, by forgetting profane
reasoning, you need only to open your eyes
to what is.

p. 69.   It turns yellow in order to bestow mystic-
ally upon the neighbouring leaf, which is red,
the harmony of the necessary note.

p. 72.   I warn you that soon I shall see you no more and that I shall turn everything against you.

But when I try to rush toward evil, may I go limping!

p. 73.   Dona Prouhèze.—Man in the arms of woman forgets God.

Guardian Angel.—Is being with him forgetting him? is one anywhere, except with Him, associated with the mystery of His creation?

Crossing again for a moment into Eden through the gate of humiliation and death?

D.P.—Is not love outside the sacrament a sin?

G.A.—Sin too!   Sin also can serve.

BIOGRAPHICAL DATES

1868   Born in Villeneuve-sur-Fère-en-Tardenois, in the department of Aisne.

1881   The family moves to Paris. Claudel studies at the lycée Louis-le-Grand.

1886   First reading of Rimbaud. Conversion in Notre-Dame, December 25, at service of Vespers.

1890   First version of *Tête d'Or*.

1892   First version of *La Jeune Fille Violaine*.

1893   First trip to United States. New York.

1894   Consul in Boston, Massachusetts.

1894–5   France. China. Second version of *Tête d'Or*.

1898   Shanghai. Second version of *La Jeune Fille Violaine*.

1900   Visit to the Benedictine monastery at Ligugé.

1901–5   Second visit to China.

1905   France. *Partage de Midi*. Marriage with Reine Sainte-Marie Perrin, March 15.

1907–14   Correspondence with Jacques Rivière.

1910   *L'Annonce faite à Marie*.

1911   Consul in Frankfurt.

1913   Consul in Hamburg.

1914   France, after expulsion from Germany.

1917   Ministre plénopotentiaire in Rio de Janeiro, with Darius Milhaud as secretary.

1919   France. Ministre plénipotentiaire in Copenhagen.

1919–24 Paris, Copenhagen, Tokyo. *Le Soulier de Satin*.

1926 Appointed ambassador to Washington.

1927–33 Washington. First exegesis of Bible: *L'Apocalypse*.

1933–35 Ambassador in Brussels. *Jeanne au Bûcher*.

1935 Retires to Brangues (Isère).

1943 First performance of *Le Soulier de Satin* at the Comédie-Française, November 27.

1946 Elected to the Académie Française.

1955 Died in Paris, on Ash Wednesday.

SELECTED BIBLIOGRAPHY

(Gallimard editions unless otherwise noted)
(*English translations)

Poetry

Cinq Grandes Odes, 1910
Corona Benignatatis Anni Dei, 1914
   **Coronal,* Pantheon Books, 1943
Poèmes de Guerre, 1915
Feuilles de Saints, 1925

Drama

Tête d'Or, 1889, 1894
   **Tête d'Or,* Yale and H. Milford, London, 1919
La Ville, 1890, 1897
   **The City,* Yale, 1920
L'Echange, 1893
Partage de Midi, 1906; Mercure de France, 1948
L'Otage, 1910
L'Annonce faite à Marie, 1910, 1912
   **Tidings brought to Mary,* Yale, 1927
Le Pain Dur, 1918
Le Père Humilié, 1920
Le Soulier de Satin, 1928–29
   **The Satin Slipper,* Sheed & Ward, 1945
Théâtre Complet, 2 vols., Bibliothèque de la Pléiade,
   1949

Writings on Holy Scripture

Les Aventures de Sophie, 1937
Introduction au Livre de Ruth, Desclée de Brouwer, 1938
Un Poète regarde la Croix, 1938
Paul Claudel interroge l'Apocalypse, Egloff, 1946
Le Livre de Job, Plon, 1946
Paul Claudel interroge Le Cantique des Cantiques, Fribourg, 1948
Emmaüs, 1949

Critical writing, essays, letters

Connaissance de l'Est, Mercure de France, 1900
L'Art Poétique, Mercure de France, 1907
Correspondance 1907–1914. Rivière et Claudel. Plon, 1926
Positions et Propositions, 2 vols., 1928, 1934
Conversations dans le Loir-et-Cher, 1929
Correspondance 1899–1926. Gide et Claudel. 1949
Correspondance 1904–1938. Suarès et Claudel. 1951

Books on Claudel

Angers, Pierre, *Commentaire à l'Art Poétique de Paul Claudel*, Mercure de France, 1949.
Barjon, Louis, *Paul Claudel*, Editions Universitaires, 1953
Fowlie, Wallace, *Clowns and Angels*, Sheed & Ward, 1943
Friche, Ernest, *Etudes Claudéliennes*, Portes de France, 1943

Madaule, Jacques, *Le Génie de Paul Claudel*, Desclée de
    Brouwer, 1933
Madaule, Jacques, *Le Drame de Paul Claudel*, Desclée
    de Brouwer, 1947.
Peyre, Henri, *Hommes et Œuvres du 20e siècle*, Corrêa,
    1938
Rivière, Jacques, *Etudes*, 1911